Contents

Text commentary – Section 5        49

Quick quiz 5        55

Text commentary – Section 6        56

Quick quiz 6        59

Writing essays on
    *Of Mice and Men*        60

Key quotations        62

Exam questions        64

Planning an essay        66

Spidergram essay plans        67

Sample response – C grade        70

Sample response – A grade        73

Quick quiz answers        76

escape. Crooks's automatic rejection of friendship or companionship is caused by the anguish of his <u>loneliness</u>. Once encouraged to do so, he reveals that he has an <u>intelligent</u> <u>awareness</u> of life. His new-found confidence and self-respect encourage him to try to counter the intrusion of Curley's wife, but he is humiliated by her vicious threats.

## Curley

Curley is a small man and seems to have developed an <u>inferiority</u> <u>complex</u> as a result. He is continually <u>aggressive</u> and constantly looking for an opportunity to assert his masculinity. <u>Humiliated</u> by his wife's apparent dissatisfaction and unhappiness, Curley needs to boost his self-esteem and confidence. His stance is that of a <u>professional</u> <u>fighter</u> – he was once a boxer – but, significantly, <u>he</u> <u>fights</u> <u>unfairly</u>. He takes advantage of those whom he thinks are weak, while carefully avoiding those he considers to be a match for him. He takes pleasure in inflicting the maximum amount of damage and pain possible, in order to dispel his frustration and anger and maintain his authority through <u>violence</u>.

## Curley's wife

Curley's wife is <u>never</u> <u>named</u> in the novel. She is not treated as an individual in her own right, but is seen by various characters as a <u>symbol</u> of other things: Curley's wife, a temptress, a chattel, a sex object, or a piece of 'jail bait'. Although she is married, <u>she</u> <u>flaunts</u> <u>herself</u> around the ranch in inappropriate clothing, flirting with the ranch-hands. She is very conscious of the effect this has on the men.

Her dreams of a better, more fulfilling life are based on glossy film magazines and cheap chat-up lines. Her ambition to work in films or in the music hall stems from her desire to be admired. This wish is partly rooted in vanity and partly in her insecurity and loneliness, much of which is brought about by her husband's inadequacies and fault-finding behaviour. We do not know how far she would pursue her assignations with the men if she were given the chance. Our only opportunity to find out occurs in her meeting with Lennie in the barn, and this is described with very skilful ambiguity by Steinbeck. Certainly her general posture and conduct is full of sensual promise.

## Slim

Slim is dignified, charismatic and a master craftsman. He exerts a natural authority with a gentleness and friendliness that contrasts with the pervasive violence that shapes the lives of the other characters. He represents a strong moral force in the novel, and acts almost like a 'conscience' to the other characters. Steinbeck's descriptions of Slim suggest an idealised characterisation, though Slim's own words and actions are convincingly realistic. Steinbeck attaches images of royalty and divinity to him: 'majesty', 'royalty', 'prince' and 'authority'.

## Candy

Candy is near to the end of his useful life on the farm and knows he has little to look forward to. The loss of his hand stresses the casual violence of the ranch-workers' lives. He also loses his dog – the only companionship he has enjoyed. However, he is given renewed comfort, strength and self-respect by the prospect of a part-ownership of the dream farm with Lennie and George.

# About the author

**John Steinbeck**

Much of *Of Mice And Men* is based upon John Steinbeck's life and experiences and his interest in contemporary social issues. He was born in 1902 at Salinas in California and graduated from Salinas High School in 1919. He went on to study English at Stanford, but left without getting a degree. In the years that followed, he had many casual jobs, varying from newspaper work to being an itinerant ranch-hand. He had some local success as a writer before *Of Mice And Men* (originally called *Something that Happened*) became an immediate and worldwide success and brought him international recognition. The publication of the novel was followed in the same year (1937) by a stage play, which won an award for the best New York play.

In the novel, Steinbeck highlights a social problem of immense proportions and of which he had experience at first hand. Climatic changes and drought in the West of America between 1880 and 1930 destroyed large tracts of fertile land which had supported the early homesteaders. These were settlers who had established the sort of small farms that represent the 'promised joy' of the workers in the story. The great financial collapse of 1929, which heralded the Depression, increased unemployment and poverty throughout the United States. White-collar and industrial workers suffered heavily, but for those who sought a living on farms the situation was doubly disastrous. Franklin D. Roosevelt's New Deal economics did much to reduce the problem, but in 1937 it was a long way from disappearing and would not fully do so until America's entry into World War II in 1941.

Itinerant American workers replaced the traditional immigrant Mexican labour in south-western states like California. They were exploited by farm owners, who employed them on low rates of pay and in appalling conditions. These men were only in demand for short periods at a time, and they had to save enough from seasonal work, such as harvesting crops and fruits, to support themselves through the rest of the year. Because they had to travel to find work, it was difficult to maintain families or roots and they often led a solitary existence. Their poor quality of life was of great concern to Steinbeck, who dealt with this problem in his novel *In Dubious Battle,* and also in his most successful book, *The Grapes of Wrath*, which won the Pulitzer Prize in 1940.

Steinbeck's novels of this time had, therefore, a grittily realistic element and also a political slant. His undoubted masterpiece, *The Grapes of Wrath*, strongly supports Roosevelt's state interference to reduce unemployment, and even reveals Communist sympathies. However, the other main influence on Steinbeck was quite different: all his life he had an uncritical devotion to the Arthurian legend. This gives *Of Mice and Men* a notable poetic element. Nobility and honour are venerated, as they were by the Knights of the Round Table, and many of his characters are on a quest, as the Knights were for the Holy Grail.

John Steinbeck is one of the finest and most successful American novelists. He received the Nobel Prize for Literature in 1962, specifically for his pre-war novels. When he died in 1969, he was America's most distinguished novelist, but it would be fair to say that for all his later success, his finest work came some 30 years earlier in his realistic/poetic response to the sufferings of the American working man.

● Find out more about John Steinbeck. Visit www.steinbeck.org/MainFrame.html

# Historical background

### Historical timeline

**1929** The great financial crash of 1929 develops into what became known as the Depression. The resulting closure of banks and factories, and the collapse of farms leads to widespread unemployment and extreme poverty.

**1931** Banks and factories close, farming collapses, unemployment and poverty are widespread.

**1933** Franklin D. Roosevelt becomes President.

**1936** New Deal – provides support for unemployed in terms of training, conservation and construction.

**1937** *Of Mice and Men* is published.

### Social impact of the Great Depression

The story of George and Lennie, while fictional, is rooted in historical fact. The high unemployment caused by the Great Depression resulted in people travelling to find work, and being hired and fired at will by powerful farm owners (like the boss in the novel). George's fear that the boss will refuse them work is therefore realistic. This should also help you to understand why the dream farm is so important to the characters. The necessarily itinerant lifestyle led to a large section of the population being fragmented, unable to put down roots, and to social instability.

### Literary tradition, realism and naturalism

The Depression provided writers and artists in the 1930s with a new way to look at what they had known as the booming America of the 1920s. There was a pervasive concern to record the difficult experiences of the ordinary human being, and Steinbeck was not alone in raising the cultural awareness of the poor conditions throughout society. The popular culture of Western magazines provided escapism from the grim realities of life on the ranch.

The social concern of writers and artists led to a movement to write and depict ordinary life as it actually was rather than to romanticise it. Steinbeck's novel is realistic, and his employment of vernacular speech helps the reader to experience the novel as the characters do.

Some writers, including Steinbeck, considered that experiences were a result of forces beyond the control of the individual. In *Of Mice and Men* it is clear that Steinbeck viewed man and nature as connected, an idea known as naturalism. At the end of the novel, Lennie's return to Salinas Pool promotes this idea.

### Further research

● www.multimedialibrary.com/FramesML/IM13/IM13:html Photographs of migrant farm workers and conditions in California. This site will help you to appreciate the social and historical context of the novel.

● Look up some of the language particular to America that Steinbeck uses: www.lausd.k12.ca.us/Belmont_HS/mice/index.html

John Malkovich and Gary Sinese in the 1992 film adaptation.

## Dreams

Many of the characters in the novel have dreams, in the sense that they have hopes or ambitions. These dreams are often kept secret to begin with. George is displeased when he discovers that Lennie and Candy have told Crooks about their secret dream farm. In contrast, Curley's wife seems almost desperate to tell Lennie about her dreams. It is ironic that she confides in someone who appears to have no interest in, or understanding of, what she is saying. Generally speaking, there is a choice of two types of dream open to the ranchers: the dream that includes companionship, honesty and love (like the dream farm idea), or the dream/nightmare of a solitary state that excludes all other human contact. George provides an example of the second kind of unhappy vision when he sees his future as unending aimless drifting: 'I'll take my fifty bucks an' I'll stay all night in some lousy cat house. Or I'll set in some pool-room till ever'body goes home.'

## Loneliness

Many of the characters are lonely, and this motivates them to look for an alternative way of life. This is one of the reasons why they are drifters: they are continually searching, often without really knowing what they are looking for. Characters are also lonely because of something within themselves, something which almost seems to make their loneliness inevitable. Different characters seek comfort and solace in different things: for Candy it is his dog; for George and Lennie it is each other; for Crooks it is his pride and his unerring skill at pitching horseshoes.

## Nature

The world of nature plays a large part in the events of the novel. Lennie is described as a 'bear', and is often surrounded by animals and the natural environment. Lennie is himself very natural in that he has an animal-like simplicity and innocence. The ranch-hands' lives are unnatural because they lead a rootless existence outside of any 'proper' society. The behaviour of human beings towards animals is echoed in the way the characters behave towards each other. Candy's dog is at the end of its useful life, and its killing is justified by some of the men because of this. If judged in the same way, the killing of Lennie may seem to be justified.

Steinbeck also uses animals to reinforce the theme of violence in the book (the snake eaten by the heron, for example). Finally, nature is shown to be full of powerful spiritual forces, as when, near the start of the book, the large carp 'sank mysteriously into the dark water again'.

## Violence

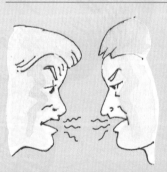

The world of the men in the book is filled with unnecessary and gratuitous violence: Candy and Crooks have been crippled, the boss permits fighting, Curley's irrational aggression, etc. Carlson is another character who seems to thrive on violence, either when he is arguing with others or when he is goading them on. The gun's easy availability – together with Carlson's unthinking but detailed explanation of his killing technique – provides George with the means to dispatch Lennie later on.

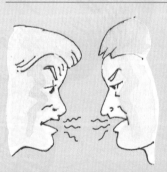
Themes and images

15

# Text commentary

## Section 1

The book opens with the suggestion that the <u>peaceful</u> <u>world</u> <u>of</u> <u>nature</u> is disturbed by man. The effect becomes more pronounced during this section as the 'sound of footsteps' grows louder and the animals flee to safety. This movement from <u>harmony to discord</u> appears in most of the natural settings in the book. Note how nature is described and relates to the action. The green pool is portrayed as an <u>idyllic</u> and beautiful place which is innocent and peaceful, rather like the <u>Garden of Eden</u>.

> **"***Guys like us, that work on ranches, are the loneliest guys in the world***"**

George and Lennie are <u>itinerant</u> <u>(wandering)</u> <u>workers</u>. They are drifters who move from ranch to ranch. They dress in the traditional manner of cowboys, from whom they descend. They are skilled in the various aspects of farm work. George and Lennie find themselves a 'few miles south of Soledad'. This is a real place in California and its name – which is Spanish – can mean <u>loneliness</u> or a lonely place.

George – 'every part of him defined' – gives an immediate impression of <u>intelligence</u>. He is reminiscent of a <u>quick-witted</u> <u>animal</u> with his <u>'restless'</u> ways. George leads the duo and we can see that he is clearly the one who is <u>in charge</u>. Both men have endured much physical hardship. George washes in the pool in traditional cowboy style. Unlike Lennie, he is a <u>cautious</u> person.

Lennie is described as a 'bear'. This animal context establishes at once the essential nature of the man – the combination of brute strength and animal-like innocence. The bear is a particularly appropriate image for Lennie, because it shares not only his harmless appearance (as of a teddy-bear), but also his dangerous tendency to hold onto things in his bear-hug.

Steinbeck suggests a great deal about Lennie by describing his movements. The unthinking way in which Lennie drinks from the 'green' pool reinforces the impression of a markedly animal temperament. Like an animal, Lennie always tries to satisfy his immediate needs and seems unable to see the possible consequences. In this case, George reminds him it was only the previous night that he was sick. One of Lennie's most dangerous failings is his inability to learn from past experience. George's admonishment establishes his role as Lennie's mentor (or keeper), with the responsibility of protecting Lennie from himself.

Lennie and George 'suit' each other because of their complementary natures. Both men are dressed the same way, but in temperament they are different: Lennie is slow, clumsy, and 'easy-going', George is quick, precise, apprehensive and cautious. Notice that it is Lennie who always seems to suffer because of his impetuous and reckless behaviour.

Some aspects of Lennie's behaviour contribute to the humour in the novel. Here, for example, the way he dips 'his whole head under, hat and all' is contrasted with George's behaviour. This reveals George's awareness that the open countryside is not without its dangers; he knows that 'You never oughta drink water when it ain't running'. This episode reinforces our impression of Lennie as being more like an animal than a man. Look at how he uses his 'paw'.

> *Lennie, who had been watching,*
> *imitated George exactly*

**Explore**

Steinbeck uses
Lennie's poor memory
as a narrative
technique. It provides
an excuse to present
the reader with
background material.

Not only is George Lennie's mentor and saviour, but clearly
Lennie looks up to him as a model of correct behaviour,
and tries to please George with his actions. Lennie is not
able to remember things easily. We are told something
about what caused the two men to be on the run from
their last employment, and this is the first suggestion that
Lennie's animal-like behaviour includes an <u>unconscious,
instinctive search for affection</u>.

Lennie's <u>'petting'</u> of small animals tells us about his need for some
sort of <u>physical contact</u>. This is an important aspect of Lennie's
character, one that is tragically resolved at the end of the book. As
the novel unfolds, notice how Lennie's fatal petting of other
creatures progresses from a dead mouse to the hoped-for rabbits,
to a puppy, and finally to Curley's wife.

Earlier, Steinbeck revealed some past trouble with 'girls', and now
we find that the two men have recently been hounded from their
previous jobs as Lennie has done <u>'bad things'</u>. The fact that Lennie
<u>'giggled'</u> at the thought of it makes the incident sound less serious
than it really was, but in fact <u>he had a close shave with death</u>.
This is an excellent narrative technique to hold the reader's
interest; Steinbeck is gradually revealing to us the
enormity of the event and its consequences.

George thinks that without Lennie he could <u>'live so easy
and maybe have a girl'</u>. This is the first example in the
book of characters dreaming of better things in the
future. Such dreams become increasingly important.

> *The flame of the sunset lifted from the*
> *mountaintops and dusk came into the valley*

**Explore**

**Notice how Steinbeck uses the natural surroundings to mirror the mood of the action.**

George appreciates the stillness and harmony of the <u>pastoral</u> scene around them. This moment of calm interrupts the interplay of the two characters and re-establishes a <u>sense</u> <u>of</u> <u>harmony</u>. It also introduces a <u>gentler</u> <u>tone</u>.

> ❝*What mouse, George? I ain't got no mouse.*❞

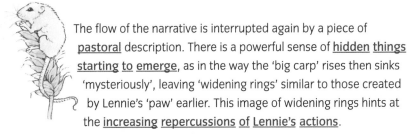

Lennie desperately needs something to pet. He is prepared to hunt around for the carcass of the mouse and is evasive and guilty when George orders him to hand it over. Steinbeck again uses animal imagery and describes Lennie as being <u>'like</u> <u>a</u> <u>terrier'</u>, a dog which, like Lennie, has a determination to <u>hold</u> <u>on</u> to things. (Notice Steinbeck's repeated use of natural similes: 'like'/'as'.) This prepares us for events to come. Lennie is reluctant to let go of the <u>mouse</u>, which he has accidentally <u>'broken'</u> by petting it. He has killed other small creatures, or <u>'pinched</u> <u>their</u> <u>heads</u> <u>a</u> <u>little'</u>, as he puts it. He wants something that is warm and alive. Lennie's behaviour will have devastating consequences in the future.

The flow of the narrative is interrupted again by a piece of <u>pastoral</u> description. There is a powerful sense of <u>hidden</u> <u>things</u> <u>starting</u> <u>to</u> <u>emerge</u>, as in the way the 'big carp' rises then sinks 'mysteriously', leaving 'widening rings' similar to those created by Lennie's 'paw' earlier. This image of widening rings hints at the <u>increasing</u> <u>repercussions</u> <u>of</u> <u>Lennie's</u> <u>actions</u>.

> ❝*God a'mighty, if I was alone I could live so easy*❞

George's frustrations with Lennie's behaviour come to a head at this point. The better life which George says he could enjoy if he did not have Lennie seems a fairly limited one: drink, food, hired women and gambling. It is the very lifestyle that the other workers find so

unsatisfying. By staying with Lennie, George actually enjoys
<u>companionship</u> and a <u>sense</u> <u>of</u> <u>responsibility</u> – rewards that are

greater than the empty experience of the common
itinerant worker about whom George keeps talking. This is
why, in spite of all his complaining, George does not strike
off on his own. It is obvious why George finds Lennie
occasionally irritating. However, Steinbeck uses various
methods to endear Lennie to the reader. The expression
that Lennie uses here, '<u>because</u> I <u>got</u> <u>you</u> ... <u>and</u> <u>you</u>
<u>got</u> <u>me</u>', is a very accurate assessment of their need for
each other.

**Explore**

The theme of
friendship occurs
through the novel.
Consider Slim's
concern for the other
characters, and
Candy's devotion to
his dog.

> **If you don' want me I can go off in the hills
> an' find a cave. I can go away any time.**

Lennie's suggestion is what a wild animal might do and is
particularly appropriate for a bear, the most dominant
animal image so far. Lennie has a strange kind of <u>animal</u>
<u>intellect</u> – an intelligence <u>based</u> <u>on</u> <u>intuition</u>. Of course,
Lennie's suggestion is not welcomed by George, not
only because Lennie would not survive (or would he?),
but because <u>George,</u> <u>despite</u> <u>his</u> <u>fits</u> <u>of</u> <u>temper,</u>
<u>actually</u> <u>needs</u> <u>Lennie</u>. George gets physical protection, a feeling
of doing something worthwhile in looking after Lennie, and a boost
to his own self-esteem because Lennie makes him feel superior.
Notice that George can also use Lennie as excuse for his own
failure to make a success of himself, and later admits this to Slim
when he confesses: 'I ain't so bright neither'.

> **First chance I get I'll give you a pup.
> Maybe you wouldn't kill it.**

**Explore**

Note Steinbeck's use
of tragic irony here.

By way of compensation for his outburst, George offers
Lennie a puppy – not knowing that it will contribute to his
later downfall. It is characteristic of the role of <u>fate</u> in the
novel that the best intentions of people produce adverse

effects. With hindsight, there seems to be a <u>tragic</u> <u>inevitability</u> in the way that these separate strands of incident and words spoken are carefully and unerringly woven together. This pervades the climax of the story.

> **❝ *Jesus Christ, somebody'd shoot you for a coyote if you was by yourself* ❞**

In the end it is George who shoots Lennie. Steinbeck <u>weaves</u> <u>his</u> <u>ideas</u> very closely together and sometimes casual remarks later turn out to carry the weight of the whole narrative.

> **❝ *We're gonna have a little house … An' live off the fatta the lan'* ❞**

Lennie enjoys George's story, just as a child enjoys a familiar fairy story, but it represents far more to both men. This is <u>'paradise'</u> or <u>'heaven'</u>, as Crooks later calls it. After killing Curley's wife, Lennie is tormented by the certainty that he has destroyed his chances of ever reaching this 'paradise'.

George briefs Lennie on what he is to say when they reach the farm and tells him to return to this place and <u>hide</u> <u>in</u> <u>the</u> <u>brush</u> <u>if</u> <u>he</u> <u>gets</u> <u>into</u> <u>trouble</u>. When this actually happens, it completes the <u>symmetry</u> of the novel. This is particularly appropriate because of the way the pool has been described as a <u>natural</u> <u>haven,</u> <u>a</u> <u>secret</u> <u>dream-like</u> <u>place</u> which is a natural sanctuary for Lennie. Bear in mind that in the Bible, Adam took refuge in a similar way from the wrath of God.

The first episode of the novel ends on a note of peace and harmony as the two men drift off to sleep and their dreams.

## Uncover the plot

1   In the passage below, select one from each set of alternatives.

Two errant/itinerant/eminent farm hands, George and Lennie, camp beside a natural pool before travelling on to a nearby ranch to find work/buy a house/live off the land. Steinbeck depicts George as small and shapeless/quick-witted/pale-eyed, responsible for the huge and nervous/restless/childlike Lennie. The two men have had to leave the town of Salinas/Soledad/Weed because Lennie unwittingly frightened a girl/mouse/rabbit there. George expresses his pride/resentment/shame at having to look after Lennie, but when Lennie offers to give him his mouse/shoot himself/leave him, he regrets his meanness. We learn that Lennie has a passion for 'petting' pretty things, especially girls/dresses/small animals, unaware of his own dangerous strength. George describes their dream of giving up work/buying a house/finding permanent work on a ranch; he tells Lennie to return to Weed/the pool/the ranch if he should get into any trouble.

## Revealing the characters

2   What does Steinbeck's physical description of George tell you about his character?

3   Where does Steinbeck use animal imagery to describe Lennie?

4   Who was the 'lady' that used to give Lennie mice?

5   Why are Lennie and George different from the other ranch workers?

## Setting the scene

6   State the effect of Steinbeck's language in each of the following quotations about setting.

(a)  'On the sand-banks the rabbits sat as quietly as little grey, sculptured stones.'

(b)  'Only the tops of the Gabilan mountains flamed with the light of the sun that had gone from the valley.'

(c)  'A big carp rose to the surface of the pool, gulped air, and then sunk mysteriously into the dark water again.'

# Section 2

The setting of the <u>bunk-house</u> is probably derived from Steinbeck's own experience as a ranch-hand. As with the novel's opening description, the technique is <u>theatrical</u>, setting the scene first and then introducing characters through dialogue. This home for the workers is very <u>sparse</u> in comforts, and contrasts strongly with the richness of nature described in the novel's opening section.

> ❝*The boss was expectin' you last night*❞

Candy's opening remark establishes the character of <u>the</u> <u>boss</u> before we meet him. We feel unease at such an immediately <u>unfriendly</u> welcome, with its hint of <u>conflict</u> and <u>intimidation</u>.

> ❝*What the hell kind of bed you giving us, anyways*❞

**Explore**

**Steinbeck emphasises the poverty of ranch life through the detailed description of the bunk-house.**

Suspecting that his bed contains <u>vermin</u>, George inspects it cautiously. As he does so, Candy chatters on about the <u>boss</u>. We learn that he <u>vents</u> <u>his</u> <u>anger</u> on the black stable-hand, provides the men with whisky and <u>allows</u> <u>a</u> <u>fight</u> between the stable-buck and 'Smitty', one of the skinners. Despite this, the boss could be worse. Candy insists he's <u>'a pretty nice fella'</u> and, after all, he keeps the two cripples on the pay-roll. We should not expect modern standards of civilised behaviour in this setting, but the atmosphere of <u>latent</u> <u>violence</u> has the potential to create trouble for (and from) Lennie.

The arrival of the boss justifies our expectations. His black clothes remind the reader of the <u>stereotyped</u> 'good' and 'bad' men in Westerns. He is a <u>proud</u> man who wears 'high-heeled boots and spurs' to accentuate his position.

> ❝*Strong as a bull*❞

Again Lennie is described in terms of an animal. This emphasises his great strength and is a further example of George unwittingly revealing the truth of things. Lennie's last name, **Small**, is ironic and amusing, an observation quickly made by Carlson.

The boss suspects that George is taking advantage of Lennie: 'You takin' his pay away from him?' As the boss begins to quiz Lennie, George breaks in loudly to help him. Is George **overprotective**, do you think? His constant interruptions serve only to arouse the boss's suspicion. George's comment that Lennie 'Damn near lost us the job' might seem rather harsh. Does Lennie provide George with something on which to vent his exasperation when things are not going to plan?

> ❝ *drag footed sheep dog, gray of muzzle, and with pale, blind old eyes* ❞

**Explore**

**Foreshadowing is one of Steinbeck's narrative devices.**

The entrance of **Candy's dog** makes us compare the harmony of nature with the aggression and confusion of the bunk-house. The dog, which is at the end of its useful life, has provided companionship for its gentle owner for many years. The **dog's death foreshadows George's killing of Lennie**.

Our first impression of Curley is complicated – his 'brown face', 'brown eyes' and 'tightly curled hair' disguise the menace in his later conduct. His glance is **cold** and he adopts the **stance of a fighter**, with his 'hands closed into fists'. Even the way he looks and moves is **threatening**. His high-heeled cowboy boots give him a status above that of the ranch-hands.

> ❝ *Let the big guy talk* ❞

A second **confrontation** is caused by Lennie's attempts to obey George's instructions to say nothing. Curley's presence does not bode well for George's and Lennie's safety. This is emphasised by Candy's comments, <u>'he's</u> <u>alla</u> <u>time</u> <u>picking</u> <u>scraps</u> <u>with</u> <u>big</u> <u>guys'</u>. Since Lennie is a bear-like giant of a man, sooner or later he <u>seems certain</u> <u>to</u> <u>provoke</u> <u>a</u> <u>violent</u> <u>assault</u> <u>from</u> <u>Curley</u>.

Curley is proud of his new wife, particularly when she makes others envious of him. Notice the implication that his hand is kept soft by the vaseline in his <u>glove</u> in order that he may 'pet' his wife. Steinbeck has already established a frightening <u>connection</u> <u>between</u> <u>Lennie,</u> <u>'petting'</u> <u>and</u> <u>death</u>, so this is <u>ominous</u>.

Is Curley's self-esteem and confidence undermined because his wife is not satisfied with their married relationship and is 'eyeing' other men? This would explain his <u>need</u> <u>to</u> <u>establish</u> <u>his</u> <u>manliness</u> with the workers. Curley seems to think that he can gain authority only by <u>physically</u> <u>terrorising</u> <u>others</u>. Why does a character like Slim not seem to need to establish his manliness in this way? We later learn that the ranch-hands despise Curley. Try to decide why. Notice that there is an <u>inverse</u> <u>relationship</u> <u>between</u> <u>size</u> <u>and</u> <u>authority</u> in some characters in the novel.

> **❝I'm scared. You gonna have trouble with that Curley guy. ❞**

George is frightened for Lennie's safety, not only because of Curley's aggression, but also because of the way Curley's wife is likely to flaunt her attractiveness. Lennie is frightened of violence, despite his great strength and size, and is not aware of his own physical strength.

## Explore

**Steinbeck himself referred to the novel as having a 'play-novelette' form and wrote that it was 'a tricky little thing designed to teach me to write for the theatre'.**

This episode is followed by a <u>description</u> of the arrival of the grain teams outside. The <u>atmosphere</u> of menace and fear is emphasised by the harsh and abrasive <u>noises</u> approaching. The success of various film adaptations of the novel owes something to a narrative style that is reminiscent of theatre and film scripts.

We now meet Curley's wife for the first time. The <u>extravagance</u> and <u>provocativeness</u> of the girl's dress and make-up make us unsympathetic towards her. Her general appearance seems completely unsuitable for life on a ranch. The dominating colour, <u>red</u>, is also <u>symbolic</u> of a woman with loose morals (as in the expression 'a scarlet woman'). She seems <u>very conscious of herself</u>, but nothing in what we are told directly about her intentions actually suggests that she is being sexually provocative.

**Explore**

Watch the film called *Of Mice and Men*, produced by MGM in 1992. Note that the director gives Curley's wife a larger role than Steinbeck does. The director also encourages the audience to have more sympathy for her than is present in the novel.

> **❝ *Gosh, she was purty* ❞**

The uncomplicated, bovine Lennie is <u>transfixed</u> by the obvious prettiness of Curley's wife. Whereas the others can see the limitations of her attractions and speculate about her morals, Lennie is conscious only of an animal awareness of the opposite sex.

George senses imminent danger and tries to warn Lennie about the kind of woman Curley's wife is. He calls her <u>'jail bait'</u>, although in fact the consequences of her contact with Lennie will be far worse than any jail sentence. Lennie intuitively senses trouble and suggests that they leave the ranch. George has to balance his <u>instinct to escape</u> against the <u>need to earn money</u>, and this need outweighs his misgivings. This decision will cost him dearly in the end.

**Explore**

Try to decide whether Curley's wife is frightened of her husband. If you think she is, why does she deliberately court disaster? Is she unwittingly provocative and ignorant of the effects of her behaviour?

On learning from Slim that Curley has gone home looking for her, Curley's wife suddenly becomes <u>nervous</u>. There is clearly some sort of <u>tension</u> between them. The suggestion is that her behaviour could be the cause.

> **❝ *He moved with a majesty only achieved by royalty and master craftsmen* ❞**

Text commentary

Slim is a man of 'majesty' and 'authority' and is capable 'of understanding beyond thought'. He is a character of strong moral principles who acts as judge and adviser in the events to come. Slim's gentle and friendly tone is in marked contrast to the harshness of the rest of the ranch and its brutal inhabitants. Unlike many others in the novel, he is not suspicious of the relationship between George and Lennie and gives them tacit approval. He shows that it is possible to command respect through natural authority rather than through bullying and violence.

Carlson is, at his first appearance, a cheerful, good-humoured man who seems to be friendly with Slim. Carlson is unsentimental about Candy's dog as he can see no further practical use for it. Although his suggestion is perhaps reasonable (that Candy shoots his dog and gets a pup instead), he seems oblivious to the strong bond between Candy and his pet. A parallel is developing between Candy's relationship with his dog, and the relationship between George and Lennie.

Slim does not respond directly to Carlson's suggestion about Candy's dog, and his delay adds suspense and, therefore, tension to the coming discussion with Candy.

Text commentary

**Explore**

Steinbeck's use of vernacular speech adds realism to the novel.

> *"Ya, know, Lennie, I'm scared I'm gonna tangle with that bastard myself. I hate his guts."*

Steinbeck does not allow any sense of security to last for long, and Curley's reappearance interrupts Lennie's delight at the prospect of owning a puppy. Steinbeck ends Section 2 with a pitiful image of the dog, who 'gazed about with mild, half-blind eyes'. The human characters, too, cannot see very far and do nothing to halt the inevitable approach of tragedy.

# Quick quiz 2

## Uncover the plot

1  In the passage below, select one from each set of alternatives.

George and Lennie arrive at the ranch. They are given
food/work/bunks by Candy, the boss/swamper/skinner, and signed up
by the boss/the boss's son/Curley. The boss is angry that they arrived
too late for the day's/weekend's/morning's work, and impressed
by/suspicious of/pleased with George's protectiveness of Lennie.
Candy/Carlson/Curley, the boss's son, is kind to/indifferent to/
antagonistic towards the new men, especially Lennie. They learn from
Candy that Curley has recently married a tart/nice girl/prostitute. The
whole set-up pleases/scares/interests George, who warns Lennie to
have nothing to do with Curley. The other ranch-hands return from
work. Slim/the stable buck/Whitey is very friendly; Carlson is more
concerned with shooting Slim's/Smitty's/Candy's old dog, and asks
Slim to give Lennie/George/Candy one of his puppies/rabbits/mice to
raise. In the midst of Lennie's excitement at the possibility of owning a
pup, Curley returns in search of his itinerant/eminent/errant wife.

## Revealing the characters

2  What is Lennie's surname, and why does Carlson find it funny?

3  Who wore 'a soiled brown Stetson hat, and … high-heeled boots and
spurs to prove he was not a labouring man'?

4  Who is 'grey of muzzle, and with pale, blind old eyes'?

5  Whose 'glance was at once calculating and pugnacious'?

6  Who is 'purty', with 'the eye' and had 'full, rouged lips and wide-
spaced eyes, heavily made up'?

7  Whose 'authority was so great that his word was taken on any
subject, be it politics or love'?

## Setting the scene

8  What is the effect of the three powerful images of sunshine?

9  Find three quotations that show how Steinbeck describes the bunk-
house to emphasise the theme of loneliness.

# Section 3

This section opens with a description of the surrounding __environment__. The 'evening brightness', so beautifully described in the first section of the book, is noticeably excluded from this scene, and the atmosphere in the bunk-house is now that of '__dusk__'. This setting maintains the sense of __foreboding__.

Slim has agreed to let Lennie have one of the puppies. It is characteristic of Slim that he makes little of the gift. We learn that __Slim killed several of the puppies at birth__, and it is crucial to understand that Slim kills the puppies for a reason, whereas Lennie does not realise what he is doing. George describes __Lennie's delight when he is given the puppy__. The description provides a __comic touch__ with the suggestion that the huge and lumbering Lennie might climb into the box with the pups.

> **Explore**
>
> **Notice how Section 2 ends with the 'ancient dog' and Section 3 opens with the new pups. Steinbeck contrasts death and life, tragedy and hope.**

66 *He damn near killed his partner buckin' barley* 99

Steinbeck continually provides hints and __premonitions of disaster__. Hardly a page goes by without some reference to Lennie's __tendency to get into trouble__. George observes that Lennie is sure to get into trouble sooner or later, 'like you always done before'. The emphasis on __Lennie's strength__ not only demonstrates Slim's generosity in praising him but also serves to prepare us for the outcome of the violence which occurs later.

66 *George fell silent. He wanted to talk. Slim ... sat back quiet and receptive.* 99

Having created the sympathetic character of Slim, Steinbeck uses the __dramatic device__ of a __conversation__ to reveal more about the relationship between George and Lennie. We learn about their origins in Auburn, Lennie's <u>Aunt</u> <u>Clara</u> and their <u>mutual</u> <u>need</u> <u>for</u> <u>companionship</u>. The story of Lennie and the <u>Sacramento</u> <u>River</u> is important for illustrating various aspects of their friendship. It shows how <u>fully</u> <u>Lennie</u> <u>trusts</u> <u>George</u> and how <u>forgiving</u> he is. What do you think it reveals about George's attitude to Lennie? Does it give any hint of why George remains loyal to Lennie?

> **❝** *He ain't mean ... I can see Lennie ain't a bit mean* **❞**

Slim's readiness to praise Lennie shows not only his <u>thoughtfulness</u> but also the <u>generosity</u> in his character. He sees <u>Lennie's</u> <u>true</u> <u>worth</u>. Slim's assessment of situations is treated like the word of God. No doubt George is proud that Lennie's true worth is appreciated by Slim. Slim also says that there is plenty of <u>violence</u> <u>in</u> <u>the</u> <u>environment</u> of the ranch and that <u>'meanness' is</u> <u>bred</u> <u>by</u> <u>isolation</u>.

We learn that George has no relations and has been saved from loneliness and perhaps from disillusionment by Lennie. Loneliness and isolation become a preoccupying theme of the novel from this point onwards, highlighting the <u>plight</u> <u>of</u> <u>the</u> <u>itinerant</u> <u>worker</u> who goes through life without putting down roots. To what extent do you think this explains the reason for George's and Lennie's partnership?

> **❝** *He jus' wanted to touch that red dress, like he wants to pet them pups all the time* **❞**

The seriousness of the <u>incident</u> <u>in</u> <u>Weed</u> is underlined by the revelation that Lennie would have been <u>'lynched'</u> (hanged) had they caught him. This foreshadows the violence of the hunt for Lennie at the end of the novel.

The colour of the girl's dress in Weed – <u>red</u> – is also ominously the dominant colour in the description of <u>Curley's wife</u>. Slim carefully considers the evidence which George gives him about Lennie. He believes George's assertion that Lennie is not dangerous and had not intended to harm the girl in Weed. However, you should notice the <u>escalation of violence in Lennie's behaviour</u> as described by George and the fact that Lennie is <u>fascinated</u> by the blatant sexuality of Curley's wife. Steinbeck uses the symbolic colour of red to warn of disaster and it is doubtful whether Lennie's state of innocence will survive, given this kind of provocation.

**❝What pup, George, I ain't got no pup ❞**

**Explore**

**Notice how this mirrors Lennie's childlike behaviour with the mouse in Section 1.**

The <u>limits of Lennie's understanding</u> are displayed when he puts the life of the puppy at risk by removing it so soon from its mother. It shows just how powerful is his <u>urge for</u> <u>'petting'</u> and how much it seems to dominate his personality.

**❝Why'n't you shoot him, Candy? ❞**

**Explore**

**Is Carlson's detachment and cool analysis of the situation harsh or justified?**

Candy and his dog have been together for so long that Candy is not aware of the dog's offensive smell. Carlson says 'he ain't no good to himself' by way of justification for killing the dog. Notice also that the way Carlson talks about Candy's dog echoes the way the stable buck, Crooks, says the ranch-hands behave towards him. In describing precisely how he will shoot the dog painlessly, even down to the exact location for the bullet, Carlson is unwittingly showing George how he will eventually dispose of Lennie. <u>Lennie is eventually shot by the same gun</u>, and in the same place in the back of the head, as Candy's dog. These <u>echoing devices</u> in the book give it a strong sense of unity.

**❝Well, you ain't bein' kind to him ❞**

With these words **Carlson** is ironically sentencing Lennie, who will later suffer the same fate as the dog. Carlson assumes that Candy can soon **get another pet** – just as he later seems to assume that George can easily **get another friend**. Carlson, like some of the other characters, does not appreciate these bonds.

**Candy and his dog** are an obvious parallel to **George and Lennie**. even the way the dog follows Candy around the same way Lennie follows George. Just as **Candy feels tied down** by his relationship with his dog, so **George feels trapped** by his sense of responsibility for Lennie.

> "*Carl's right, Candy. That dog ain't no good to himself. I wisht somebody'd shoot me if I got old an' a cripple*"

Slim's opinions are valued by all the ranchers and his pronouncement about Candy's dog seals its fate. By appealing to others to do the same for him if he should ever get old and a cripple, **Slim paves the way for the killing of Lennie**, who is mentally crippled. Slim's considered verdict has **the force of law** on the ranch.

Steinbeck increases the **tension** and **suspense** generated by the proposal to shoot the dog by the episode with **Whit**, a character who remains undeveloped. The episode, which shows him excited by an item in a **magazine**, slows down the pace of the action and serves to illustrate the **poverty of experience and education** known by most of the ranch-hands.

> "*He led the dog out into the darkness*"

Carlson is not a cowboy, but does possess a hand-gun. The conversation about the **gun** lets George know where it is kept. It is the sensitive Slim who points out that Carlson will need a shovel in order to give the dog a decent burial. Steinbeck emphasises the **long wait** by mentioning muted

Explore

Notice Steinbeck's use of nature to accompany the dog's death and the similar setting when Lennie is shot at dusk in Section 6.

sounds, like 'shuffle', 'rippled' and 'gnawing', which contrast with the eventual 'shot'.

> ❝*That big new guy's messin' around your pups out in the barn*❞

Immediately after the dog's death we are reminded of Lennie and his obsessions by Crooks's comment (above). George's words a few lines further on, 'If that crazy bastard's foolin' around', ring with **double** **meaning**, for the words **'foolin' around'** are usually applied in America to intimate behaviour between males and females. Later on, it will be Curley's wife – and her seeming desire to 'fool around' with the ranch-hands – who preoccupies George.

Whit uses the name of **Candy's dog** – Lulu – to describe **Curley's wife**. His description of her 'concealing nothing' and giving everyone the 'eye', coming straight after the description of Lennie's behaviour with the dogs in the barn, emphasises Lennie's innate ability to get into trouble. It is unfortunate that George and Lennie have arrived at a moment when trouble seems likely to erupt. Steinbeck builds the tension and expectation towards a climax which will fuse together all these different elements.

You should consider the fix that George finds himself in. He says of Curley's wife, 'She's gonna make a mess', so why doesn't he move out at once to avoid trouble? **Whit underlines the basic predicament of itinerant workers:** their existence is mean and centres around violence, cheap sex, drinking and fighting. They earn insufficient money to be able to save up and build a 'stake' for a more deeply satisfying life. Why is it that they always spend their money on 'blackjack' and 'whores', as Crooks observes in Section 4? Consider the extent to which their desire for carefree enjoyment and pleasure is the 'serpent' in their Garden of Eden.

**Carlson** may be practical and have the cold nerve necessary to kill the dog, but he is fairly **callous** too. He makes no effort to conceal the cleaning of the recently fired gun from Candy, who must find the sound of the snapping of the ejector a painful reminder of his dog's death.

The killing of Candy's dog is an interesting example of the technique which Steinbeck is trying out in this book, which is a cross between a <u>novel</u> and a <u>play</u> or drama. Each of the <u>six sections</u> (actually split into chapters in some editions) deals with one <u>scene</u>. Each <u>opens</u> <u>with</u> <u>a</u> <u>description</u> of the scene and is <u>followed</u> <u>by</u> <u>dialogue</u> between characters who <u>enter</u> and <u>exit</u> in the same way that they would in a play or film.

**Explore**

**How effective is Steinbeck's play/novel technique, do you think? Why do you think he experimented with this way of writing? Think about how effective this method is in helping the reader to imagine the events and the conversations which take place.**

If you look carefully you will notice that almost every piece of description or storytelling is like a <u>stage</u> <u>direction</u> to a theatre or film director. Each section (or chapter) could easily be translated into an act or scene on stage, as indeed happened when the book was first performed as a play (in November 1937). In Steinbeck's own adaptation, the dialogue was changed very little. Another thing which should remind you of a playscript is that <u>very</u> <u>few</u> <u>characters</u> are used – far fewer than in most novels. The <u>length</u> is also significant. The stage version runs for around two hours. It is hardly necessary to make any cuts at all, which is probably unique in novel adaptations for the stage.

Consider the impact that the <u>development</u> <u>of</u> <u>cinema</u> may have had on literature of this time. (*Of Mice and Men* was written in 1937.)

> ❝*Curley burst into the room excitedly*❞

Curley is clearly looking for a <u>victim</u> on whom he can <u>vent</u> <u>his</u> <u>frustration</u> <u>and</u> <u>anger</u>. He demands to know where Slim is. Presumably he suspects him to be a rival for the affections of his wife. Slim is a <u>mysterious</u> and potentially dangerous character. He has a genuinely caring nature and his reason for going out to the barn is typical of him – he makes a special point of dealing with the mule's

Text commentary

injury himself. He has a strong presence whenever he appears, and is a <u>powerful figure of authority</u>.

As a typical ranch-hand, <u>Whit</u> is eager to witness or participate in any brawling. He encourages George to go out to witness the possible confrontation. George wants to stay out of trouble and avoid getting the sack. The <u>choice</u> between leaving the ranch or staying to earn a stake becomes increasingly vital. George is <u>torn</u> between the need to protect Lennie and the fulfilment of his dream of a homestead. He wants more from life than the Whits and Carlsons of the ranch world – he has clear and definite ambitions.

George seems to have a <u>very biased and basic view of women,</u> which was not unusual for the time of the novel. He sees them only as instruments to relieve certain physical urges, as a device to <u>'get ever'thing outa his system all at once, an' no messes'</u>. He does not express the need for any female companionship beyond this, and his <u>lack of trust</u> is further illustrated by the fact that women do not feature in his dream of a smallholding. This may indicate that, in spite of his relationship with Lennie, George fears a deep and loving relationship.

> 66 *George, how long's it gonna be till we get that little place an' live on the fatta the lan'?* 99

Is the farm just a dream? George talks wistfully about his mental picture of the farm. He sits <u>'entranced with his own picture'</u>. George's dream-like description <u>slows down the pace</u> of the novel at this point and provides a period of 'pastoral' <u>calm before the storm</u>. The life and surroundings which George imagines are the very opposite of his present existence. His life, and Lennie's, would be more closely related to nature on his dream farm – as he says, 'when we put in a crop, why we'd be there to take the crop up', so the cycle of the natural <u>rhythms of nature</u> would be

complete. The situation sounds so much like a dream that it comes as something of a surprise to the reader to learn that **the place does in fact exist**, and is not just a bedtime story thought up to amuse Lennie. This makes George's need for a stake easier to understand.

> ❝*Nobody never gets to heaven, and nobody gets no land* ❞

Man's longing for a piece of **land** was a **favourite theme** of Steinbeck's, and he returned to it in nearly every novel he wrote. Although you can see several particular examples of personal tragedy in *Of Mice And Men*, Steinbeck clearly also means the story to be a **parable of the human condition.** In the poem from which the novel's title is taken, Burns wrote that **'the best laid schemes o' mice an' men gang aft a-gley'**. The phrase 'gang aft a-gley' literally means 'go often astray', but Steinbeck does not translate Burns's 'aft' as 'often', but instead as 'always'. As Crooks says: **'Nobody never gets to heaven, and nobody gets no land.'** All the characters' plans go astray: not just George and Lennie's, but those of Curley, his wife, Crooks and Candy. What other reasons can you think of for the choice of title?

George suddenly realises that what has been until this point only a distant dream is now a **real possibility** with Candy's involvement and contribution. Candy's savings offer them all **the prospect of self-respect and companionship**. The characters have a **moment of hope** before being plunged straight into conflict. The ranch-hands' shared sense of euphoria and of the **beauty of the dream** is in stark contrast to the surroundings in which they actually find themselves.

> ❝*I ought to of shot that dog myself, George. I shouldn't of let no stranger shoot my dog.* ❞

Candy seems to feel that he has shown a lack of courage in not shooting his dog himself, and with this admission the dream of the men is broken.

Slim and Curley enter. Curley's suspicions have proved to be groundless and he is trying to apologise. This seems likely only to increase his **humiliation** and his feelings of **frustration** and **anger**. Carlson remarks that Curley should make his wife stay home, if he doesn't like her wandering round the ranch. This serves to **aggravate Curley's rising temper**, with devastating consequences. The way Curley moves from man to man, getting insults and jokes thrown at him, indicates that Carlson's assessment of his character is probably correct. He does seem to be a **coward**, despite his notoriously violent streak.

Carlson seems to enjoy deliberately making the situation with Curley worse because he is confident of his own ability to handle any resulting violence. Candy also enjoys joining in the attack on Curley. Although he is only one-handed – and therefore in no position to defend himself physically – Candy is in the company of George, Slim and Carlson, and so is safe from attack. Unfortunately, this leaves **Lennie exposed as a target**.

**❝No big son-of-a-bitch is gonna laugh at me.
I'll show ya who's yella.❞**

It is typical of Curley that he should **pick on Lennie** for his display of violence. In picking on the large but apparently harmless man, Curley demonstrates his own **cowardice**.

There is an **irony** in the fact that it is **Lennie's happy thoughts** about the farm that leave a smile on his face. The smile is **misinterpreted** by Curley. Despite his size, Lennie has two distinct disadvantages: he will not act unless commanded to by George, and he is terrified by aggression. Because of this he does not make any attempt to defend himself. Curley is a vicious fighter and is out to inflict grave damage on Lennie, who needs George to trigger his reaction. Notice the use of animal imagery here: Lennie stands like a **'bear'** with 'paws' covering his face, but Curley is **'the dirty little rat'**. Lennie's immense strength and tenacious grip crush Curley's hand. This is not aggression but more of a **reflex action**.

> **Suddenly Lennie let go of his hold**

This shows the extent of the responsibility that George carries for Lennie's actions. Lennie is **almost uncontrollable** and it takes a great deal of effort on George's part to penetrate Lennie's fear and first get him to defend himself and then to release his grip on Curley's hand.

> **It ain't your fault ... This punk sure had it comin' to him. But – Jesus! He ain't hardly got no han' left.**

Slim's **surprise and horror** give greater emphasis to Lennie's strength and the damage which he is capable of causing. Although Curley has got what he deserved, Slim still has enough **compassion** to take care of the injured man and assumes the **responsibility** of getting him to a doctor. Slim is definitely master of the situation and has the **shrewdness** to manipulate the situation to George's and Lennie's advantage. He turns Curley's pride against him, and suggests that if the truth about the fight were to become known, Curley would become a laughing stock.

> **Lennie was jus' scairt ... He didn't know what to do. I told you nobody ought never to fight him.**

George's **worst fears are beginning to come true**. In his single-minded pursuit of a stake, and in his deliberate disregard for the danger of their situation and its probable consequences for Lennie, he is risking a **dreadful calamity**.

# Uncover the plot

1   *Delete two of the three alternatives given, to find the correct plot.*

*Section 3 opens at morning/noon/dusk, signalling the foreboding to come. George thanks Slim for giving Lennie one of his puppies, and tells Slim what happened at the pool/in Weed/in the barn. With the tacit permission/disapproval/scorn of Slim, Carlson shoots Candy's old dog. While Curley is out in the barn accusing Lennie/George/Slim of 'messing' with his wife, George and Lennie tell Whit/Candy/Crooks that they are planning to buy a plot of land that George has seen; Candy offers to swamp the farm/tend the rabbits/put up some money towards it if they will include him. Curley returns, mistakes Lennie's smile of delight at the new developments/his puppy/Curley's wife for derision, and picks a fight with him. At George's command, Lennie crushes Curley's hand.*

# Revealing the characters

2   *Why does George confide in Slim about the incident in Weed?*

3   *What three character attributes are revealed about Slim in this section?*

4   *How does Steinbeck foreshadow George's shooting of Lennie at the end of the novel?*

5   *Why is Carlson so eager to shoot Candy's dog?*

6   *Describe Curley's feelings about Slim.*

7   *Why does Curley pick on Lennie?*

8   *Why does Lennie fight back?*

9   *How does Slim prevent Curley from getting Lennie and George fired?*

10  *How does Candy feel about the shooting of his dog?*

# Setting the scene

11  *How does Steinbeck describe the natural setting during the shooting of Candy's dog?*

# Section 4

Section 4 opens with a description of the **harness** **room** of the stables. It would be easy to construct a **stage** **set** from the detailed instructions given.

As Crooks's name suggests, he is crooked in the spine as a result of an accident. He is not an itinerant worker like the others and this **room** **represents** **home**. Crooks is supposed to be **exceptional** in that he is **literate** and **conscious** **of** **his** **rights**. His 'Large gold-rimmed spectacles' and the 'mauled copy of the California civil code for 1905' are **symbols** **of** **his** **learning**. He is in constant pain and treats himself, as he does the horses, with liniment. This is the **private** **act** **of** **a** **private** **man** – he is therefore understandably annoyed at the interruption from Lennie. Much of Crooks's pride and truculence is a **defence** **against** **the** **racial** **prejudice** he experiences from the other ranch-hands. He has been **excluded** by the inhabitants of the bunk-house because of his colour.

> ❝*Ever'body went into town ... Slim an' George an' ever'body.*❞

You might think it very foolhardy of George not to stay behind to keep an eye on Lennie. However, for Steinbeck, it may have been **essential** **for** **the** **development** of the story to get rid of most of the hands, in order to allow the **physical** **cripples** **(Crooks** **and** **Candy)** and the **mental** **cripple** **(Lennie)** to get together without fear of interruption.

> ❝*Why ain't you wanted?*❞

Lennie's attitude gives Crooks little reason to feel antagonised. His usual defence against the white ranch-hands is to remain 'aloof', but he seems to recognise in Lennie a genuine, uncomplicated and open nature that offers friendship without any hidden conditions or threats.

Candy has remained behind at the ranch, excited by the prospects that the new farm has suddenly opened up for him. He sees the farm as an <u>escape</u>. George has suggested that Candy should take care of Lennie on the farm, and he takes this offer very seriously. This will also help Candy to cope with the loss of his dog, and subtly reinforces the idea of Lennie as a large and gentle animal which needs supervision and care.

Lennie seems quite articulate about the prospect of living 'on the fatta the lan', although we know that he is only repeating what has often been said to him. Nonetheless, you may be surprised by the way Lennie is able to express himself. The idea of the <u>farm begins to attract Crooks</u> and he invites Lennie to sit down.

Crooks is by nature <u>proud and reserved</u>, but he is also lonely, and he decides that he can tell Lennie secrets which will not then be revealed or turned against him. We learn that he grew up enjoying a comparatively high status and standard of living. Blacks were rare in California and in this area of Soledad, so his family have been the <u>victims of prejudice</u>. The isolation which this produced was made worse by the disapproval of Crooks's father for his white friends. Crooks suggests that George and Lennie are partners because of the <u>unspoken companionship</u> of simply staying with each other.

> ❝S'pose he gets killed or hurt so he can't come back❞

Crooks seems unable to resist a rare opportunity to <u>inflict pain</u> on another person. He is usually the victim. Crooks's suggestion to Lennie is <u>vindictive</u> and <u>heartless</u>. Notice how his <u>'face lighted with pleasure in his torture'</u>. With George away, Lennie has no defence against this attack.

Lennie is alarmed by what Crooks says: 'Suddenly Lennie's eyes centred and grew quiet'. This incident shows us that, under certain circumstances, Lennie can be roused. We get a better idea of the sheer size of George's responsibility and of Lennie's helplessness.

ooks's quiet 'Maybe you can see now...' reveals the **thos** of his loneliness and isolation. Crooks **craves companionship** because he knows that human contact acts as a **confirmation** of what a person thinks and believes. Without regular contact with other people, Crooks feels that **'he got nothing to measure by'**.

> ❝*Just like heaven. Ever'body wants a little piece of lan'.*❞

Crooks is rather **scornful of the dream** as Lennie explains it to him: 'You're nuts'. In some ways Crooks has put his enforced isolation to good use, and what he says contains some useful thoughts about life in general. Crooks compares **human hopes with religious belief**. He has a fairly **cynical** view of both.

> ❝*This's the first time I ever been in his room*❞

Crooks is **disappointed** when his new friendship with Lennie is threatened by **Candy's intrusion**. At the same time he is pleased and excited at the **unusual prospect of company and a friendly evening**. Notice how Lennie innocently disregards the fact that this is Crooks's private room, while Candy is acutely aware of the social distance between himself and Crooks. With Candy, the age-old prejudices of race have prevented him from ever getting to know Crooks. It takes the innocent actions of Lennie to bring the two men together. Part of Lennie's function in the book is to act as a **catalyst** in the relationships between other characters.

> ❝*Seems like ever' guy got land in his head*❞

The conversation soon turns to the topic of the <u>farm</u>. In spite of his desperate need to accumulate money quickly, George has gone 'out on the town' with the others. Crooks's reflections about the way the itinerant workers never end up with anything seems to contain a considerable amount of truth. Candy's outburst here: <u>'Sure they all want it'</u>, contains an idea that is central to the whole book. Owning their own land, with the opportunity to see the seasons through the whole year, would give status and self-esteem to the low-paid workers.

Crooks thinks the chances of their successfully achieving their dream farm are remote. Yet they do seem so near, with only one month's further savings necessary. This <u>closeness to achieving their goal</u> contributes to the novel's final sense of <u>tragedy</u>.

Despite his cynicism, <u>Crooks is drawn into the same dream</u> of a better life and of companionship. During this brief episode he has moved from sullen resentment at the intrusion of others to <u>companionable excitement</u>. The proud isolation and prickliness we saw earlier are clearly a protective façade to conceal his frustration and loneliness.

> ❝*Any you boys seen Curley?*❞

The description of Curley's wife emphasises her <u>sensuousness</u>. Isolated on the ranch, she is also <u>lonely</u> and looking for company. Curley has abandoned his wife for a visit to a <u>brothel</u>. Does this explain the viciousness of her attacks on those others who have been left behind. Is she, like them, some sort of <u>'weak one'</u>? Is she sure herself why she behaves the way she does?

> ❝*Lennie watched her, fascinated*❞

Notice how Lennie responds to Curley's wife's obvious sexuality whenever she appears. Throughout this episode, <u>Lennie remains transfixed</u> by her.

## " Jus' the ol' one-two "

Curley's wife flares up and tells them how Curly spends all his time in the house talking about what he is going to do to **'guys he don't like, and he don't like nobody'**. This reinforces what we already know about Curley. He seems **obsessed by a need to establish his supremacy over others** (like an animal) and, presumably, his **ownership** of his wife is another facet of this. She is yet another character who craves companionship, but in her case, her sex and her husband are obstacles to her search for friendship. She seems to need to captivate men, as if she needs reassurance of the effect she has on them.

Curley's wife mirrors the ranch-hands in her loneliness and in her dream of a better life. She is evidently of limited intelligence. Apart from her unsatisfactory marriage to the boss's son, her claim to superiority comes from the fact that **'a guy tol' me he could put me in pitchers'** (already, in the 1930s, a cliché and a chat-up line to deceive the gullible).

## " And she looked longest at Lennie, until he dropped his eyes in embarrassment "

The way Curley's wife talks to Lennie has sexual undertones. **She is attracted by someone who can beat Curley**. Why do you think this is?

Lennie does not understand the double meaning in Curley's wife's words, but Crooks does and he **tries to protect Lennie**. We have not seen him assert himself in this way before, but by attempting to confront Curley's wife – a white woman – **he is putting himself at great risk**. Crooks has gained **confidence** by the open nature of Lennie and the friendliness of Candy. Steinbeck is pointing out how people become **stronger through the support and companionship of others**.

> **"I could get you strung up on a tree so easy it ain't even funny"**

All Crooks's strength is taken away by what Curley's wife says. She <u>re-establishes</u> <u>the</u> <u>brutal</u> <u>power</u> <u>of</u> <u>white</u> <u>over</u> <u>black</u>. Her <u>threat</u> of framing Crooks, alleging sexual interference, would certainly be sufficient to get him hanged. This episode prepares you for the immediate <u>rough</u> <u>justice</u> <u>of</u> <u>the</u> <u>lynch-mob</u> that pursues Lennie at the end of the novel.

Throughout this section Lennie has shown a <u>growing</u> <u>sense</u> <u>of</u> <u>confidence</u> as Crooks, Candy and he all share their dreams. Now, the outburst from Curley's wife reduces him to the state of <u>a</u> <u>helpless</u> <u>child</u>. Notice how Steinbeck uses the word 'whined' to underline the <u>animal</u> <u>imagery</u>.

The reappearance of the old prejudices makes Crooks withdraw into himself again. His response to oppression is to return to the way he was: <u>'reduced</u> <u>himself</u> <u>to</u> <u>nothing'</u>.

> **"What you doin' in Crooks's room. You hadn't ought to be in here."**

On his return, George shows annoyance at Lennie for being in Crooks's room. He is also cross at Candy because he wanted to keep the farm a secret. Crooks returns to rubbing his back with liniment. This takes us back to the opening of the scene and is another example of Steinbeck's frequent use of <u>repeated</u> <u>patterns</u> <u>and</u> <u>cycles</u>. For Crooks, nothing has changed.

# Quick quiz 4

## Uncover the plot

**1** *Delete two of the three alternatives given, to find the correct plot.*

Steinbeck opens the section with a detailed description of <u>the bunk-house/the Salinas River/the harness room</u>. All the men go <u>into town/to bed/to work</u> on <u>Monday/Friday/Saturday</u> night. Crooks, Lennie and Candy remain at the ranch. <u>Lennie/Candy/Curley's wife</u> is the first character to enter Crooks's room. Crooks <u>enjoys/resents/welcomes</u> the interruption. Lennie tells Crooks about <u>Curley/Weed/the dream farm</u> and Crooks is attracted by the prospect. Crooks <u>taunts/flatters/hates</u> Lennie. Candy joins them and the three <u>lonely/happy/sad</u> men discuss the dream farm. They are interrupted by Curley's wife, who shows special interest in <u>Crooks/Lennie/Candy</u> when she guesses that it was he who hurt Curley's hand. Curley's wife <u>threatens/teases/flirts with</u> Crooks. George returns and is <u>overjoyed/annoyed/resentful</u> that George and Candy have shared the dream farm with Crooks.

## Revealing the characters

**2** *Why is Crooks isolated?*

**3** *What does Crooks have that no other worker on the ranch has?*

**4** *Why does Lennie talk to Crooks?*

**5** *Why does Crooks taunt Lennie about George getting hurt and not coming back to the ranch?*

**6** *How does Lennie respond to the idea of George not coming back and why?*

**7** *How does Candy feel about the dream farm?*

**8** *Why does Curley's wife interrupt the three men?*

## Setting the scene

**9** *What is different between Steinbeck's description of the bunk-house and the description of Crooks's room?*

# Section 5

This section again starts with <u>evocative</u> <u>scene-setting</u>. Notice how Steinbeck appeals to the reader's sense of <u>hearing</u> as well as <u>sight</u>. The visual detail is supported by the <u>onomatopoeia</u>: the sound of the word echoes the sense of 'nibble', 'wisp', 'stamped', 'bit', 'rattled', 'buzz' and 'humming'. It all creates a warm and lazy atmosphere. Noises made by the men outside – 'clang', 'shouts', 'jeering' – intrude on the quiet atmosphere. The barn is a <u>fitting</u> <u>environment</u> <u>for</u> <u>the</u> <u>gentle</u> <u>and</u> <u>uncomplicated</u> <u>nature</u> <u>of</u> <u>Lennie</u>.

> ❝*Lennie sat in the hay and looked at a little dead puppy that lay in front of him* ❞

Lennie has killed the puppy by clumsily petting it. His tendency to inflict <u>damage</u> <u>through</u> <u>trying</u> <u>to</u> <u>show</u> <u>love</u> is becoming more pronounced. There is a moment of great <u>pathos</u> when he 'unburies' the puppy. He is struggling to come to terms with what he has done and particularly with his <u>disobedience</u>. The <u>inner</u> <u>turmoil</u> that this misfortune has caused prepares us for the coming scene with Curley's wife. Steinbeck has created a <u>tragic</u> and <u>doom-laden</u> atmosphere in which we are very aware of Lennie's <u>instability</u>.

Curley's wife is attracted to Lennie because he has got the better of her husband. She has worked out a complicated arrangement to ensure that she can safely be alone with him in the barn without interruption. Appropriately, she wears a 'bright cotton dress' and 'red ostrich feathers'. We know already how strongly Lennie is attracted to the colour <u>red</u>.

Lennie is particularly <u>vulnerable</u> here because of his <u>unhappiness</u>. He is <u>mourning</u> the death of the puppy and is <u>terrified</u> that it may have robbed him of any chance of the dream farm. This makes him receptive to the offer of companionship and consolation, in spite of George's previous warnings to stay away from Curley's wife and not to talk to her.

The description of the death of the puppy foreshadows what is about to happen to Curley's wife. This incident tells us more about her character – we see her vulnerable side and her humanity in consoling Lennie – but it also gives the scene tension and a high potential for danger.

> " *Why can't I talk to you? I never get to talk to nobody. I get awful lonely.* "

**Explore**

Steinbeck has used this technique of 'almost-soliloquy' before. Think back to the conversation Crooks had with Lennie in the harness room.

Curley keeps his wife on a tight rein. When she does get the chance to talk to someone, the words pour out of her in a 'passion of communication'. In what almost amounts to a soliloquy (because Lennie really isn't paying any attention to most of what she says), Curley's wife reveals her own dreams of a better life. Notice how her dream parallels that of Candy, Crooks and George. Curley's wife seems to be star-struck and to have taken seriously the flattering promises made by men trying to ingratiate themselves with her. Despite her attempts at sophistication, she seems pathetically naive, notably when she is convinced that her 'ol' lady' stole the letter from Hollywood. Although she mocks the men's dream, underneath she is no different from them. Think again about George's judgement of her as 'jail bait'. Was he fair, do you think?

Curley met his wife at a dance hall, one evening when she had decided that she could not stay at home any longer. His offer of marriage was her last chance of escape. However, she 'don' like Curley'.

**Explore**

Compare Lennie's incapacity for judgement with Slim, who consciously avoids judging people.

As was the case with Crooks, Lennie's innocent and open manner inspires confidence here. Curley's wife finds her 'dream' in the glittery world of show-business, the cinema and glossy magazines. This is in sharp contrast to that of the three men. Her interest in the world of cinema and film stars suggest that her behaviour and clothes are designed to provoke interest and attention rather than to invite intimacy. Despite her sensuality and provocative appearance, she seems only to want to talk to Lennie.

## 66I like to pet nice things 99

Lennie has moved from mice to the puppy and thence to dreams of owning rabbits. Lennie explains that what attracted him to the rabbits he saw at a fair was their long hair. This aids our understanding of the transition from rabbits to Curley's wife.

To begin with, Curley's wife has been content to snuggle up to Lennie, but now she begins to be alarmed by his obsession with petting. Nevertheless, she still underestimates the danger in Lennie's behaviour and her own closeness to him. She describes him as a big baby.

## 66Curley's wife laughed at him 99

This is a difficult moment in the book to understand. How deliberate, do you think, is Curley's wife's suggestion that Lennie might fondle her hair? She could be innocently referring to its texture, or knowingly leading Lennie towards a sexual encounter. Her intentions at this moment are crucial in allocating blame for what happens next, but they remain unknown. We cannot be certain whether she was in the barn just to talk companionably to Lennie, or whether she was intent upon seduction. Notice how she only struggles when her appearance is 'mussed up', which is consistent with her vanity.

## 66Lennie was in a panic. His face was contorted. 99

Lennie's panic gives rise to the use of <u>physical</u> <u>force</u> and the results, as with the puppy, are <u>fatal</u>. It is important to notice that the reason for Lennie's panic and anger is his <u>fear</u> <u>that</u> <u>George</u> <u>may</u> <u>discover</u> that he has broken his promise. George uses the threat of the loss of the dream farm and the rabbits to keep Lennie under control.

## 66 *I done another bad thing* 99

Although Lennie says he has done another 'bad thing', we are never sure that he fully grasps its significance. Lennie is <u>far</u> <u>more</u> <u>worried</u> <u>that</u> <u>what</u> <u>he</u> <u>has</u> <u>done</u> <u>will</u> <u>make</u> <u>George</u> <u>cross</u>. Steinbeck uses the word 'pawed' here to remind you of the animal imagery which always accompanies Lennie. More evidence of <u>Lennie's</u> <u>inability</u> <u>to</u> <u>tell</u> <u>good</u> <u>from</u> <u>bad</u> is that he leaves Curley's wife to go and conceal the puppy's body, because he thinks that its death will make things worse for him. Lennie has <u>no</u> <u>in-built</u> <u>sense</u> <u>that</u> <u>people</u> <u>are</u> <u>any</u> <u>more</u> <u>important</u> <u>than</u> <u>other</u> <u>animals</u>. Notice how Lennie's neglect has the effect of making the death of Curley's wife even sadder.

## 66 *As happens sometimes, a moment settled* 99

This <u>lyrical,</u> <u>descriptive</u> <u>passage</u> emphasises the contrast with the violence of the drama that has just taken place. The scene is set at <u>dusk,</u> and the sounds that Steinbeck mentions are more <u>distant</u> and <u>harmonious</u>. The dog that comes in reminds the reader of Lennie's <u>lost</u> <u>animal</u> <u>state</u> <u>of</u> <u>innocence</u>. By her death, Curley's wife is also returned to a <u>natural</u> <u>state</u> <u>of</u> <u>innocence</u>.

Steinbeck's writing technique is very similar to <u>script-writing</u> <u>for</u> <u>the</u> <u>cinema</u>. We have seen how carefully he constructs settings for each main section of the book and only then introduces the characters. Here he introduces what in a film might be a kind of <u>freeze-frame</u>. This device creates a <u>quiet</u> <u>moment</u> before the turbulence of the conclusion of the story.

As the action resumes, it is <u>ironic</u> that it should be Candy who enters since he has been working out more details of the farm which may have been Lennie's salvation. All their hopes are dashed by his discovery of the body. Notice how Steinbeck uses <u>sound</u> to accompany the restarting of the action: the noises get louder, from 'stamped' and 'chinked' to 'stamped and snorted', 'chewed' and 'clashed'.

> **❝❝I should of knew❞❞**

George has been removed from the action for about 30 pages, and now he reappears. This has given Lennie the freedom to behave without George's guiding and restraining hand. George confesses that what has happened is <u>what he feared all along</u>. His thoughts are immediately for Lennie. Candy, who is much more realistic now, says that the ranch-hands, led by Curley, will exact their own kind of brutal justice.

> **❝❝You an' me can get that little place, can't we George?❞❞**

Candy's 'greatest fear' is that the <u>farm is now gone</u>. George realises that his own prospects are now no better than those of all the other itinerant workers, with their <u>limited aspirations</u> of cheap sex and gambling.

> **❝❝such a nice fella❞❞**

Circumstance and the quirks of Lennie's character have brought about this <u>tragic conclusion</u>. George says that Lennie was never motivated by malice and that the victims are just <u>casualties of his innocence</u>. Candy's bitter attack on Curley's wife hints at her symbolic role – through her action of <u>'messing things up'</u> he and his friends have lost their dream and the chance of a new life.

Slim examines the body and confirms that Curley's wife is dead. Everyone respects his authority as the leader of the group. Even allowing for Curley's emotional reaction, you should still notice that the basis of <u>Slim's</u> <u>authority</u> <u>is</u> <u>a</u> <u>quiet</u> <u>firmness</u>, while <u>Curley's</u> <u>instinct</u> <u>is</u> <u>always</u> <u>towards</u> <u>instant</u> <u>violence</u>.

The prospect of a <u>man-hunt</u> and the opportunity to use his Luger excites <u>Carlson</u>, who seems to want to solve all his problems with his <u>gun</u>. His keenness to use his Luger on Lennie reminds us of his former enthusiasm to use it on Candy's dog.

Curley's response is <u>aggressive</u>, probably because he already has a score to settle with Lennie. Rather than let the law take its course, Curley announces his intention of <u>shooting</u> <u>Lennie</u> <u>in</u> <u>the</u> <u>stomach</u> with a shot-gun. This would lead to a very <u>slow</u> <u>and</u> <u>painful</u> <u>death</u>.

George does all he can to get the men to promise that they will take Lennie alive and not harm him. However, from the way Curley treats the search as a <u>hunt</u> <u>for</u> <u>an</u> <u>animal</u>, saying he will <u>'shoot</u> <u>for</u> <u>the</u> <u>guts'</u> by way of revenge, George can tell there would be no hope of Lennie coming out of it alive. He directs the hunters the wrong way.

Slim is as <u>perceptive</u> as usual, and realises that to catch Lennie alive and lock him up would not really be the answer. He talks about Lennie's capture as if Lennie were a wild animal. Slim seems to be suggesting that the <u>most</u> <u>humane</u> <u>way</u> <u>to</u> <u>treat</u> <u>Lennie</u> <u>would</u> <u>be</u> <u>to</u> <u>kill</u> <u>him</u>: 'Curley's gonna want to shoot 'im … An' s'pose they lock him up an' strap him down and put him in a cage. That ain't no good, George.' As ever, Slim's word is law.

**Explore**

Notice how this echoes Slim's comments about Candy's dog in Section 3.

## Uncover the plot

1   *Delete two of the three alternatives given, to find the correct plot.*

   *The setting of this section is <u>the barn/the ranch house/the Salinas River</u>. It is <u>Saturday/Sunday/Monday</u> afternoon when Curley's wife finds Lennie in the barn, grieving for the puppy he has inadvertently killed. <u>Without her permission/At her invitation/Despite her warning</u>, Lennie touches her hair; she panics and Lennie, terrified by her <u>silence/tears/screams</u>, breaks her neck. Remembering George's instructions, Lennie returns to <u>the north/Weed/the pool</u>. <u>Curley/George/Candy</u> discovers the body and realises their dream is over. He fetches George, who sends the other men the <u>wrong way/after Lennie/to Soledad</u> while he goes to find Lennie.*

## Revealing the characters

2   *What are Lennie's feelings about the puppy he has killed?*

3   *Why does Curley's wife want to talk to Lennie?*

4   *What is her dream?*

5   *How does Curley's wife feel about Curley?*

6   *Why does she suggest to Lennie that he touches her hair?*

7   *Why does Lennie put his hand over her mouth?*

8   *Does Lennie realise the full extent of what he has done to Curley's wife?*

9   *Why does he hide the puppy's body?*

10  *Why is Candy upset at the end of the section?*

11  *What does Slim think about Lennie when he sees the body?*

12  *What does George decide to do and why?*

## Setting the scene

13  *Why does Steinbeck open the section with the setting of the barn?*

# Section 6

This final section <u>returns</u> <u>to</u> <u>the</u> <u>opening</u> <u>setting</u>. In a way that echoes the shooting of Candy's dog, Lennie has been taken outside by Steinbeck into the <u>natural</u> <u>world</u> where he belongs and where he is to die. It is useful to compare both descriptions of the Salinas River. The <u>pastoral</u> <u>calm</u> <u>is</u> <u>still</u> <u>noticeable</u>, but the action of the <u>heron</u> here in swallowing the little water snake hints at the <u>violence</u> <u>in</u> <u>nature</u>. The silence of the original setting is disturbed by the 'gust' of the wind and the <u>noise</u> of the leaves, which occurred only at the very end of the opening scene.

By ending the novel where it began, Steinbeck brings the action of the book <u>full</u> <u>circle</u>. This gives a feeling of completeness to the story, but does it give you the same feeling about the lives of the characters? We are left with the feeling that they are forever <u>doomed</u> to wander from farm to farm, from casual acquaintance to casual acquaintance, endlessly repeating the <u>hopeless</u> <u>cycle</u> of their lives.

> *he came as silently as a creeping bear moves*

The description of Lennie drinking at the pool parallels that in the opening section. This time, instead of throwing himself into the water, he drinks as a real <u>hunted</u> <u>animal</u> might, cautiously, alert for every sound. Notice how the other animals in the clearing all move away.

> *And then from out of Lennie's head*

Steinbeck again uses a <u>film</u> <u>technique</u> to illustrate the <u>complex</u> <u>nature</u> <u>of</u> <u>Lennie's</u> <u>mentality</u>. His guilt and its consequences are played out in a scene between Aunt Clara (his former guardian) and himself. <u>Aunt</u> <u>Clara</u> <u>is</u> <u>the</u> <u>character</u> <u>of</u> <u>George</u> and says what George would say – although, interestingly, not with his voice.

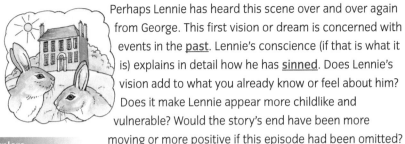

Perhaps Lennie has heard this scene over and over again from George. This first vision or dream is concerned with events in the <u>past</u>. Lennie's conscience (if that is what it is) explains in detail how he has <u>sinned</u>. Does Lennie's vision add to what you already know or feel about him? Does it make Lennie appear more childlike and vulnerable? Would the story's end have been more moving or more positive if this episode had been omitted?

**Explore**

Make sure you can explain *why* you feel the way you do about Steinbeck's use of this unusual device.

The appearance of the giant rabbit is to do with Lennie's <u>fear</u> <u>for</u> <u>the</u> <u>future</u>. The rabbit is a <u>symbol</u> of a time of peace in quiet and natural surroundings, both in the past of childhood (toy rabbits) and in the future of the dream farm. Lennie tells himself that this dream has been shattered by events. He seems to be gaining some grasp of the implications of what has happened, although he has to conjure up imaginary beings to explain. This device gives you an insight not only into <u>what</u> <u>Lennie</u> <u>thinks</u>, but also <u>the</u> <u>way</u> <u>he</u> <u>thinks</u>.

The next passage – which begins 'Only the topmost ridges' – is almost identical to a section near the start of the book, except that this time the distant sounds of men are no longer incidental and unimportant, but indicate the whereabouts of the hunting party.

George arrives. To reassure Lennie, he moves through <u>familiar</u> <u>exchanges</u> to a point where they begin to talk once more about how they have each other for support and companionship. Steinbeck conveys George's <u>anguish</u> with light touches here and there, using words and phrases like 'he said woodenly', 'quiet for a moment', 'shakily'. George also speaks to Lennie <u>calmly</u> <u>and</u> <u>quietly</u>, without his usual outbursts, calling him by his name instead of the more usual 'crazy bastard' and 'son-of-a-bitch', which he uses when he is angry. George has rarely been as <u>gentle</u> as this with Lennie. On which other occasions does he treat him with equal consideration?

Text commentary

> *From the distance came the sound of men shouting at one another*

As the hunting party draws nearer, the dream farm takes on the characteristics of **heaven** and becomes a place where Lennie will find peace. George has stolen Carlson's Luger and has come prepared for this final act of **friendship**. He asks Lennie to remove his hat, thus exposing the back of his head to the bullet in the same place Carlson used with **Candy's dog**. Dreaming of the **future**, Lennie **dies happily and unsuspectingly**

Slim understands what George has done and why. He also seems to sense what it has cost George. In contrast, Carlson's question – the final words in the book – summarise the harsh world in which the characters live – a world of callousness and brutality. They are unable to understand the world of George and Slim, because they cannot see the basis upon which it is built. Curley and Carlson are not even aware of their own loneliness.

Consider whether you feel that the ending of the story was **inevitable**, or whether it might have been possible for George and Lennie to have succeeded in owning their own farm. Does the book offer any redeeming or hopeful view of the itinerants' relationships with each other? Think about whether Steinbeck offers any future for them or any possibility of happiness.

## Uncover the plot

1   *Delete two of the three alternatives given, to find the correct plot.*

*Steinbeck closes the novel with the setting of Soledad/Weed/the Salinas River to mirror the opening of the novel. The heron swallowing the water snake prefigures/follows/undermines the final, climactic, violent action. Lennie appears and swims in/stands by/drinks at the pool as the animals come near/flee/surround him. Lennie has nightmares/visions/blackouts that reflect his past and his future. When George finds Lennie he is very angry/distressed/gentle and describes their dream farm. George can hear shots/the hunting party/herons as he tells Lennie to face him/run away/turn around. Visualising their dream farm, Lennie is shot with Carlson's gun.*

## Revealing the characters

2   *How does Steinbeck describe Lennie's movements?*

3   *What are the two visions that Lennie has?*

4   *What does Lennie's first vision represent?*

5   *What does Lennie's second vision represent?*

6   *Do you think that George knows he will shoot Lennie?*

7   *Why do you think George is not angry with Lennie as he was in the opening section?*

8   *Why does George describe the dream farm?*

9   *Does Lennie die hating George?*

10  *Why do you think Carlson does not understand George at the end of the novel but Slim does?*

11  *Why do you think Steinbeck ends the novel with Carlson's lack of understanding?*

## Setting the scene

12  *Why does Steinbeck begin and end the novel with the setting of the Salinas River? What is different about the Salinas River at the end of the novel compared with the beginning?*

# Writing essays on *Of Mice and Men*

Examiners will mark your coursework essay according to four **assessment objectives** (AOs).

- **AO1:** respond critically, sensitively and in detail, selecting appropriate ways to convey response, using textual evidence.

- Remember that the text has been constructed by an author for a purpose. Do not write about the novel as if its characters and events were real. You should also write in a formal style.

- **AO2:** explore how language, structure and forms contribute to meanings of texts, considering different approaches to texts and alternative interpretations.

- Discuss the meaning of the quotations you use (evaluation of language). Show that you understand why Steinbeck organises the novel in this way, and demonstrate that there can be different opinions about the novel.

- **AO3:** there are marks available for how well you structure your sentences, your spelling and your grammatical accuracy.

- **AO4:** relate texts to social, cultural and historical contexts and literary traditions.

- Demonstrate your knowledge that Steinbeck was writing about the 1930s and the experience of the itinerant workers. You should also be able to bring into your essay the fact that Steinbeck's novel was a social commentary of the time and that this was his interest.

These Assessment Objectives also apply for examinations on *Of Mice and Men*.

There are two levels for English Literature: foundation and higher. The difference is that foundation papers will often give you a question followed by bullet points to show what you should include in your answer. You should use this as a basis for your plan. Higher papers will often give you a quotation and then a question. You should use the quotation as a starting point and then make sure you offer your own opinion.

- If you are following the AQA/OCR/WJC examination boards they may give you an extract from the novel and ask a question. Remember to show how it relates to the novel as a whole.

- At all times you must answer the question! Examiners cannot give you marks for answers that do not relate to the question. If you practise planning (for revision, make plans of past examination questions), you will ensure that you do not waste your time in the exam by writing about something that is not relevant.

- If you plan your work effectively, you will have time in the examination to think carefully about the words you write and the order you write them in.

- **Check with your teacher whether you are allowed to take in your copy of the novel and whether you are allowed to have annotations in it.**

# Key quotations

> **Guys like us, that work on ranches, are the loneliest guys in the world. They got no family. They don't belong to no place.**

Steinbeck's comment on the social conditions of ranch workers in the 1930s shows his sympathy and understanding of the world they inhabit.

> **I tell ya a guy gets too lonely an' he gets sick.**

Steinbeck draws three lonely men together to show the value of friendship.

> **Why can't I talk to you? I never get to talk to nobody. I get awful lonely.**

Steinbeck shows that even Curley's wife suffers from loneliness.

> **That mouse ain't fresh, Lennie; and besides, you've broken it pettin' it.**

Steinbeck foreshadows Lennie's killing of both the puppy and of Curley's wife, and shows that Lennie likes to pet soft things but does not know his own strength.

> **He was so scairt he couldn't let go of that dress. And he's so God damn strong, you know.**

George's revelation to Slim about the incident in Weed foreshadows Lennie's action of breaking Curley's wife's neck. We realise that he does it because he is scared and this prepares the reader to understand Lennie's final action.

> **" And then she was still, for Lennie had broken her neck. "**

Steinbeck relates the incident with simplicity and peacefulness, showing that Lennie had no intention of killing her.

> **" He pulled the trigger. The crash of the shot rolled up the hills and rolled down again. "**

George's necessary action is conveyed with simplicity.

> **" Suddenly Lennie appeared out of the brush, and he came as silently as a creeping bear moves. "**

Here, animal imagery shows Lennie as hunted.

> **" "Someday – we're gonna get the jack together and we're gonna have a little house and a couple of acres an' a cow and some pigs and —" "An' live off the fatta the lan'." "**

The natural images in the dream show Steinbeck's belief in the importance of man's connection with the environment that surrounds him.

> **" I think I knowed we'd never do her. He usta like to hear about it so much I got to thinking maybe we would. "**

George realises that the dream is dead.

# Exam questions

1. What is your opinion of Curley's wife? In your answer you should consider:

   • What she says and does.

   • What others say about her.

2. 'Well, I think Curley's married ... a tart.' What is your own view of Curley's wife?

3. 'Guys like us, that work on ranches, are the loneliest guys in the world.' says George. Explore Steinbeck's use of loneliness in the novel as a whole.

4. 'That dog ain't no good to himself. I wish't somebody'd shoot me if I got old an' a cripple.' says Slim. Discuss the importance of Candy's dog in relation to the novel as a whole.

5. 'I ain't takin' it away jus' for meanness. That mouse ain't fresh, Lennie; and besides, you've broke it pettin' it.' says George. How does Steinbeck use the device of foreshadowing throughout Of Mice and Men to alert the reader to the tragedy at the end of the novel?

6. It has been said that Of Mice and Men is sad but not entirely pessimistic. Do you think Steinbeck shows any hope or optimism about life in the novel?

7. Explore how Steinbeck uses the dream of the farm throughout the novel.

8. 'An whatta I got?' George went on furiously. 'I got you! ... You do bad things and I got to get you out.' Explore Steinbeck's presentation of George's relationship with Lennie. Why does he stay with Lennie?

9  Discuss whether you think George can be described as a hero or not.

10  Steinbeck describes Crooks as a 'proud, aloof man. He kept his distance and demanded that other people kept theirs'. Explore the character of Crooks and his importance in the novel as a whole.

11  What is the importance of the dreams the characters have in the novel?

12  Discuss Steinbeck's use of the natural settings in the novel.

13  Critics have said that Of Mice and Men has intense dramatic qualities. How far would you agree?

14  How effective is Steinbeck's use of animal imagery in the novel?

15  Of Mice and Men has been said to have a dramatic quality. Discuss the techniques Steinbeck uses to achieve this effect.

16  How and why does Steinbeck make friendship an important theme in the novel?

17  Which character in the novel do you have the most sympathy for and why?

18  How effectively do you think Steinbeck is at conveying a realistic experience of the migrant worker in 1930s America?

19  Steinbeck describes Slim as having an 'authority so great that his word was taken on any subject, be it politics or love' and that he had an 'understanding beyond thought'. Discuss the significance of Slim in the novel.

**Planning saves time!** Mapping responses means you are not thinking up ideas at the same time as trying to write. Planning will also help you to focus on answering the question.

With **coursework** plans, allow more planning time, build in more exploration of the text and more quotations. Conduct research so that your essay includes comments on social and historical context and other people's opinions.

With **exam** plans, concentrate on mapping the structure of your response and on the quality of your expression.

### Planning techniques

- *Spidergrams.* Place the essay title in the middle of the page and use a different line for each key point. Try to have about four or five key points. For each key point, have a line to show textual evidence. From the textual evidence, have a line to show evaluation of language. You can then label each line to show where it will come in your essay.

- *Tables.* These are useful for comparison essays.

- *Bullet points.* Some students learn best in a logical, ordered format and number their points.

### Essay plan checklist

1. Break down the question.

2. Brainstorm your ideas.

3. Choose your textual evidence.

4. Structure your argument: point, evidence, evaluation.

5. Check your plan.

6. Use your plan.

**What is your view of the way Steinbeck ends the novel?**

**1**
- The ending mirrors the beginning: effective structure.
  - 'the sun had left the valley to go climbing up the slopes of the Galiban Mountains'
  - The darkness adds foreboding, the dream has failed and Lennie has to die.

**2**
- Steinbeck successfully uses the natural world to mirror the actions of the characters.
  - 'the beak swallowed the little snake'
  - Steinbeck uses omens throughout the novel – this symbolises Lennie's death.

**3**
- Steinbeck uses visions to show how the reader feels about his actions.
  - 'You never give a thought to George'
    - This shows us that Lenny realises the burden he is to George and how strong their friendship is.

**4**
- The gigantic rabbit represents Lennie's fear for the future.
  - 'He gonna leave ya all alone'
  - Lennie is distraught about the rabbits, but the thing that hurts him most is the idea that he will lose George. Steinbeck reinforces the importance and value of friendship.

**5**
- Although Lennie cannot survive the laws of society, he dies knowing the strength and worth of friendship.
  - 'We got each other, that's what, that gives a hoot in hell about us.'
  - Steinbeck closes the novel with pathos and recognition that even though Lennie's fate is tragic, the friendship he shares with George is rare and priceless.

Central question: '... if I was alone I could live so easy. I could get a job an' work, an' no trouble' says George. Why do you think he does not do this?

**1** Loneliness is a major theme in the novel. All characters experience it in varying degrees.

- 'Guys like us ... are the loneliest guys in the world.'
- George repeats this phrase throughout the novel to emphasise the truth about the ranch workers' lives.

**2** Life for ranch workers: 1930s era of Depression. Life was difficult and living conditions poor.

- 'What the hell kind of bed you giving us, anyways.'
- Steinbeck describes the poor conditions of the bunk-house with the idea that George's bed has lice and ticks.

**3** Trouble: incident in Weed/losing jobs/Lennie's simplicity gets him into trouble. Foreshadows future tragedy.

- 'you keep me in hot water all the time'
- Steinbeck reveals George's torrent of anger about Lennie in a monologue at the opening of the novel.

**4** Friendship: protect Lennie/promised Aunt Clara/he used to tease Lennie/Lennie never took offense

- 'because I got you to look after me, and you got me to look after you'
- Lennie's simple statement is the basis for friendship and Steinbeck shows that even someone as simple as Lennie is capable of great friendship.

**5** George: heroic. Final act of shooting his friend is the most difficult thing he could ever do.

- 'Ain't gonna be no more trouble. Nobody gonna get hurt.'
- George's anger in Section 1 is paralleled with his desire for Lennie to die with dignity and with the dream in his mind.

## What is the significance of the title of the novel?

**1**
- Robert Burns' poem, 'To A Mouse', shows how men's dreams and future plans often go wrong, bringing tragedy.
  - 'The best laid schemes o' mice and men, / Gang aft agley.'
  - George's and Lennie's dream of the farm is shared by many ranch workers.

**2**
- Mice: symbolic in the novel. Parallel between Lennie Small and the mice he kills. Burns shows that men are helpless when pitted against society and fate.
  - 'Sure they all want it. Everybody wants a little bit of land.'
  - George's and Lennie's dream is shared by Candy and then by Crooks. The mice Lennie kills foreshadow how the dream farm falls.

**3**
- Steinbeck lets the hope build up to engage the reader. They think it can be real.
  - 'This thing they had never really believed in was coming true.'
  - Raising expectations makes the final outcome of the novel even more tragic and the reader sympathises strongly.

**4**
- Death of Curley's wife signifies the loss of the dream, hinted out throughout by omens. This causes Candy's sorrow.
  - 'His eyes blinded with tears and he turned and went weakly out of the barn…'
  - Candy has lost more than his dog, he has also lost his strength to carry on. He has nothing to look forward to.

**5**
- George loses the one person he cared about through an horrific action.
  - 'No, Lennie, I ain't mad, I ain't never ben mad, an' I ain't now. That's a thing I want ya to know.'
  - Steinbeck uses the title to show how men's dreams bring heartache and misery. However, it is also uplifting because it shows the strength of friendship.

# Sample response

'Explore the significance of the character of Crooks.'

We get a description of Crooks in the second section where Steinbeck describes him as having a 'crooked back where a horse kicked him. The boss gives him hell when he's mad.' ✓ So, this already shows that the other ranchers are not very nice to him and treat him disrespectfully. ✓✓ He is the target for when the boss is angry. They also called him a nigger, 'ya see the stable's buck's a nigger,' and Steinbeck shows that the men at the ranch are racist and discriminate ✓ against him, but we know that this was a common view in the time that Steinbeck was writing the novel. ✓✓ Even though Steinbeck does not focus on Crooks very much in the novel, he adds to the theme of loneliness. ✓

The men at the ranch do not normally let Crooks join in the celebrations. We know this because Candy says 'They let the nigger come in that night.' ✓ so obviously they do not like him and would prefer not to have him there. ✓ Candy also tells George that 'If he coulda used his feet, Smitty says he woulda killed the nigger' ✓ and this shows us that Crooks is physically attacked and noone thinks very much of it at all. ✓

Some of the words used to describe Crooks are 'Negro', 'pain' and 'patient'. ✓ I think that Crooks is a lot like the other men on the ranch because he is lonely and has nobody else to talk to ✓ and this is shown when we are told that he reads a lot. It is clear that Crooks tries to disguise ✓ his loneliness in his books and this makes him happier than he would be without them, also he lives in a stable so nobody else is around him. ✓ Later in the novel, Steinbeck tells us that he is the only man on the ranch to be able to have possessions ✓ and this makes him different to the other men on the ranch. ✓

Crooks is linked to Lennie because he also is a target for violence. ✓✓ Curley picks on Lennie because he is not very bright and is an easy target. ✓ This is similar to Crooks but it is Crooks's colour, not his lack of intelligence that makes him a target. Other people on the ranch suffer from violence too, like Candy who loses his best friend, his dog, because Carlson shoots him. ✓✓ So all three characters, Crooks, Candy and Lennie have suffered violence in their life because of other people's opinions. ✓✓

I think Steinbeck shows the reader how unjust people can be towards each other ✓ and the effect that this injustice has on others. ✓ When Lennie enters Crooks's room, his motive is that he is lonely ✓ because everyone else, except Candy, has gone into town. Lennie does not understand about racism and wants to talk. Crooks is very off with Lennie at first and then he begins to enjoy the company. ✓ Crooks is not used to company and Steinbeck describes him as a 'proud and aloof'. ✓ This means that he has dignity and he keeps his distance from everyone else. ✓✓ When Lennie tells Crooks about the farm. At first Crooks thinks he is joking, but then he gets excited and wants to join in. ✓

Steinbeck shows the reader that friendship is a powerful thing ✓

and that it can bring hope for people who have never had it. ✓✓
When Curley's wife comes into Crooks's room, she makes Crooks
remember that he is the lowest of the low. ✓ He tells Candy to
forget about including him in the dream farm and goes into
himself again and is lonely. ✓

It is as if Steinbeck gives Crooks hope for a little while and then
shows how hatred can take hope away. ✓✓ After this, each
character realises that the dream can never exist, Lennie first, then
Candy, then George.

---

### Examiner's comments

*This is, on the whole, a good response. The candidate
shows an understanding of Steinbeck's use of language
and uses appropriate quotations to support the points
made. The answer relates the themes shown through
Crooks's character to the other themes in the novel and
demonstrates awareness of cultural and social contexts,
such as racism and itinerant workers. The candidate
uses appropriate language, paragraphs and sentence
structures, and writes about the novel as constructed by
an author.*

# Sample response

'Explore the significance of the character of Crooks.'

Central to Steinbeck's novel is man's need for companionship to protect against the isolation that George recognises will lead to 'meanness'. ✔ Friendship is rare for itinerant workers in 1930s America and Steinbeck believed that the inability to put down roots led men into loneliness and isolation. ✔✔ At the core of the novel is the friendship between George and Lennie, and Crooks's role in the novel is to highlight how someone who has been isolated for most of his adult life can be restored through friendship. ✔✔ Steinbeck's creation of Crooks is the most extreme example of loneliness and epitomises the isolation of man as a result of prejudice. ✔

Crooks gets his name from an accident with a horse which has made his back crooked. ✔ The fact that he is known by this name rather than his real name highlights his lack of identity and how he is defined through an act of violence. ✔✔ Candy also tells us that Crooks is a 'nigger' and this term was commonly used at the time Steinbeck was writing. ✔ The reader learns that he is a victim of racial prejudice ✔ and this means that he is isolated ✔ from the other ranch workers. He is just one of the characters who experiences loneliness. ✔

The section of the novel where Lennie enters Crooks's room shows how loneliness can draw people together. ✔ Steinbeck describes it so precisely that it is like a set-piece from a stage play. ✔✔ It was unusual for a black person to be able to read at that time and this shows us that Steinbeck believed in education for everyone. ✔

Because Crooks lives in the stables, he has possessions that the other ranch workers cannot have. He tells Lennie 'This here's my room. Nobody got any right in here but me.' This shows us that Crooks is very protective about his space and the few rights that a black man would have at that time are precious to him. ✓✓ Lennie's simplistic view of life means that he does not recognise the social boundaries and tries to make friends with Crooks. ✓ At first Crooks is hostile towards Lennie, but realises that Lennie is so simple that he does not understand why someone would be isolated because of their colour. ✓ Crooks understands the importance of friendship and I think that he could be jealous of the friendship between George and Lennie. ✓✓ I think this is why he taunts Lennie and because he has never had the power to taunt anyone else before. ✓

Steinbeck continues with the theme of loneliness ✓ and Crooks says that 'A guy needs somebody – to be near him ... a guy gets too lonely an' he gets sick.' ✓ This is why Crooks begins to enjoy Lennie's company. ✓ When Candy joins the pair, Steinbeck, for a brief moment, allows the three 'weak ones' companionship. ✓ Crooks is very realistic and states that 'ever' guy got land in his head' ✓ and he does not believe that the farm is possible. ✓ When he realises that Candy has the money he offers to work for nothing on the farm. This shows how desperate men were to be able to put down roots and support themselves. ✓ In this section, the dream of the farm becomes a reality for all three characters, and this is what makes the novel so tragic because they all believe in it for a little while. ✓✓

It is the entrance of Curley's wife which makes Crooks realise the impossibility of achieving the dream. ✓ She reminds him who he is and of his low position. ✓ Steinbeck shows us how friendship can make someone believe in themselves, and Crooks tells her to leave. ✓ She responds by saying 'I could get you strung up on a tree so easy it ain't even funny.' ✓ It is prejudice that destroys Crooks's dreams and hopes of friendship. ✓✓ Steinbeck describes how Crooks 'reduced himself to nothing'. ✓ Crooks is the first character who states that the dream farm is simply a dream ✓ in the world he lives in and that he cannot escape. ✓ He lies and tells Candy that he 'wouldn' want to go no place like that'. ✓✓ This is what is so tragic about the story, that in the time Steinbeck was writing, he could not see any hope for the characters. ✓✓

Examiner's comments

*The candidate shows a sensitive and engaged response to the text and writes with knowledge and understanding of the 1930s context. Key points are supported with focused textual evidence and the candidate explores the meaning of Steinbeck's language and form. The candidate offers their own ideas about the meaning of the character and draws comparisons between the character of Crooks and the other characters in the novel. The response is in a suitable style and conveys ideas logically and clearly.*

# Quick quiz answers

## Quick quiz 1

1  Two <u>itinerant</u> farm hands, George and Lennie, camp beside a natural pool in a valley before travelling on to a nearby ranch to <u>find work</u>. Steinbeck depicts George as small and <u>quick-witted</u>, responsible for the huge and <u>childlike</u> Lennie. The two men have had to leave the town of <u>Weed</u> because Lennie unwittingly frightened a <u>girl</u> there. George expresses his <u>resentment</u> at having to look after Lennie, but when Lennie offers to <u>leave him</u>, he regrets his meanness. We learn that Lennie has a passion for 'petting' pretty things, especially <u>small animals</u>, unaware of his own dangerous strength. George describes their dream of <u>buying a house</u> he tells Lennie to return to <u>Weed/ the pool</u> if he should get into any trouble.

2  George is a sharply intelligent and astute man.

3  throughout the novel, but notably at the introduction to Lennie's character: 'the way a bear drags his paws', 'Lennie dabbled his big paw'

4  Lennie's Aunt Clara

5  George and Lennie's bond of friendship and their dream of the farm protects them from the loneliness and isolation.

6 (a) Steinbeck emphasises the harmony, beauty and innocence of the natural world. The simile has ironic connotations as stones are inert rather than living.

(b) The powerful and intense beauty of the scenery mirrors the strength and goodness in the relationship between the two men.

(c) Steinbeck's use of 'mysteriously' suggests that not everything in nature can be understood or rationalised.

## Quick quiz 2

1  George and Lennie arrive at the ranch. They are given <u>bunks</u> by Candy, the <u>swamper</u> and signed up by the <u>boss</u>. The boss is angry that they arrived too late for the <u>morning's</u> work, and <u>suspicious of</u> George's protectiveness of Lennie. <u>Curley</u>, the boss's son, is <u>antagonistic</u> towards the new men, especially Lennie. They learn from Candy that Curley has recently married a <u>tart</u>. The whole set-up <u>scares</u> George, who warns Lennie to have nothing to do with Curley. The other ranch-hands return from work. <u>Slim</u> is very friendly; Carlson is more concerned with shooting <u>Candy's</u> old dog, and asks Slim to give <u>Candy</u> one of his <u>puppies</u> to raise. In the midst of Lennie's excitement at the possibility of owning a pup, Curley returns in search of his <u>errant</u> wife.

2  His surname is Small. This is funny because Lennie is huge.

3    the boss
4    Candy's dog
5    Curley's
6    Curley's wife
7    Slim's
8    The movement of the sun outside creates a sense of time passing and of life going on outside the bunk-house. The atmosphere in the bunk-house is generally dark ('dusk'), foreshadowing 'trouble'.
9    '…apple box with the opening forward so that it made two shelves for the personal belongings…'
     'In the middle of the room stood a big square table littered with playing cards'
     'He studied the solitaire hand that was upside down to him.'

## Quick quiz 3

1    Section 3 opens at <u>dusk,</u> signalling the foreboding to come. George thanks Slim for giving Lennie one of his puppies, and tells Slim what happened <u>in Weed</u>. With the tacit <u>permission</u> of Slim, Carlson shoots Candy's old dog. While Curley is out in the barn accusing <u>Slim</u> of 'messing' with his wife, George and Lennie tell <u>Candy</u> that they are planning to buy a plot of land that George has seen; Candy offers to <u>put up some money towards it</u> if they will include him. Curley returns, mistakes Lennie's smile of delight at <u>the new</u>

<u>developments</u> for derision, and picks a fight with him. At George's command, Lennie crushes Curley's hand.

2    Slim's character inspires confidence and he is complimentary about Lennie.
3    Choose from: trustworthy, kind, gentle, authoritative, majestic.
4    Through the shooting of Candy's dog, who is old and crippled and no good to himself or to Candy.
5    because he smells, although he also says that the dog is in pain
6    Curley feels resentful and angry towards Slim and his natural authority.
7    Curley believes Lennie is laughing at him.
8    because George tells him to
9    Slim threatens to make Curley a laughing stock if he gets lennie and George fired.
10   Candy regrets letting a stranger shoot his dog and thinks he should have done it himself.
11   Carlson leads the dog out into the darkness. Steinbeck increases the dramatic tension of the moment through the silence which exists outside the bunk-house.

## Quick quiz 4

1    Steinbeck opens the section with a detailed description of <u>the harness room</u>. All the men go <u>into town</u> on <u>Saturday</u> night. Crooks, Lennie and Candy remain at the ranch. <u>Lennie</u> is the first character to enter

*Crooks's room. Crooks resents the interruption. Lennie tells Crooks about the dream farm and Crooks is attracted by the prospect. Crooks taunts Lennie. Candy joins them and the three lonely men discuss the dream farm. They are interrupted by Curley's wife, who shows special interest in Lennie when she guesses that it was he who hurt Curley's hand. Curley's wife threatens Crooks. George returns and is annoyed that George and Candy have shared the dream farm with Crooks.*

2  because of racial prejudice
3  a home, because he does not travel to find work
4  because he is lonely and is oblivious to prejudice (racial or any other kind)
5  *Because he realises that Lennie is more vulnerable than he is. It is a rare chance to exert power.*
6  *He does not understand that Crooks is taunting him and becomes angry at the prospect that someone may hurt George.*
7  *It is Candy's last hope.*
8  *She is lonely and wants attention.*
9  *The bunk-house only has two shelves for personal possessions. Crooks's room has a 'number of personal possessions' like several pairs of shoes, books and magazines.*

Quick quiz 5

1  *The setting of this section is the barn. It is Sunday afternoon when Curley's wife finds Lennie in the barn, grieving for the puppy he has inadvertently killed. At her invitation, Lennie touches her hair; she panics and Lennie, terrified by her screams, breaks her neck. Remembering George's instructions, Lennie returns to the pool. Candy discovers the body and realises their dream is over. He fetches George, who sends the other men the wrong way while he goes to find Lennie.*

2  *He does not understand why the puppy died and is sad. When he realises that George will be angry and won't let him tend any rabbits he gets angry.*

3  *She is curious about Lennie because he broke Curley's hand, and she says that she is 'awful lonely'.*

4  to be in the movies
5  *She says that she 'don't like Curley. He ain't a nice fella'.*
6  *She is vain and enjoys the attention*
7  *He does not want George to hear her screaming.*
8  *First he is 'bewildered' and then frightened. He may not fully understand what he has done or how he has done it, but he knows that it is a bad thing and that George will be angry.*
9  *because he thinks if George sees the puppy and Curley's*

wife he will be even more angry
10   because he knows that the
       dream farm can never happen
11   He realises that Lennie would
       not have meant to break her
       neck and that they have to go
       and get him.
12   George sends the men the
       wrong way and decides he has
       to shoot Lennie because if the
       hunting party get him they will
       torture him.
13   The barn is a rustic, natural
       setting. Its simplicity echoes the
       simple nature of Lennie.

## Quick quiz 6

1    Steinbeck closes the novel with
       the setting of the _Salinas River_
       to mirror the opening of the
       novel. The heron swallowing the
       water snake _prefigures_ the final,
       climactic, violent action. Lennie
       appears and _drinks at_ the pool
       as the animals _flee_. Lennie has
       _visions_ that reflect his past and
       his future. When George finds
       Lennie he is _gentle_ and describes
       their dream farm. George can
       hear _the hunting party_ as he
       tells Lennie to _turn around_.
       Visualising their dream farm,
       Lennie is shot with Carlson's
       gun.
2    '... as a creeping bear moves'
3    He has a vision of his Aunt Clara
       and a giant rabbit.
4    The first vision represents his
       past and his limited conscience.
       Aunt Clara represents Lennie's

friendship with George and the
painful knowledge that he has
made life difficult for his friend.
5    The second vision represents
       the death of Lennie's future.
6    Yes. George has purposefully
       taken Carlson's gun.
7    George realises that he cannot
       protect Lennie from the society
       they live in or from himself and
       this makes him sad.
8    He wants Lennie to die thinking
       of the future, of the dream.
9    No, he dies knowing that
       George is not mad at him and
       that he wants everyone to be
       nice to him and that there will
       be no more trouble.
10   Carlson does not understand
       the importance of friendship.
       Slim understands because he is
       the moral conscience of the
       novel and has an 'understanding
       beyond thought'.
11   The ending is deliberately
       tragic.
12   The symmetry of the novel
       shows the cycle of life and
       death and that man always
       returns to nature. The setting is
       different at the end because the
       water-snake is eaten by the
       heron and a gust of wind blows.
       These changes signify the onset
       of danger for Lennie.

Page 10, John Steinbeck, © Bettmann/Corbis
Page 15, Scene, © Cooper Andrew/Corbis Sygma

Design and illustration © Letts Educational Ltd

ISBN 978 1 84315 312 2

First published 1994
06/060611

Published by Letts Educational Ltd.
An imprint of HarperCollins*Publishers*
77–85 Fulham Palace Road
London W6 8JB

Text © John Mahoney and Stewart Martin 1994
2004 edition revised by Cherie Rowe

British Library Cataloguing in Publication Data.
A CIP record of this book is available from the British Library.

Cover and text design by Hardlines Ltd., Charlbury, Oxfordshire.
Typeset by Letterpart Ltd., Reigate, Surrey.
Graphic illustration by Beehive Illustration, Cirencester, Gloucestershire.
Commissioned by Cassandra Birmingham
Editorial project management by Vicky Butt
Printed in China